NEXT
LEVEL
SALES
COACHING

NEXT LEVEL SALES COACHING

HOW TO BUILD A SALES TEAM THAT STAYS, SELLS, AND SUCCEEDS

STEVE JOHNSON

MATTHEW HAWK

WILEY

Library of Congress Cataloging-in-Publication Data is Available.

ISBN 9781119685487 (Hardcover)
ISBN 9781119685494 (ePDF)
ISBN 9781119685425 (ePub)

Cover Design: Wiley
Cover Image: © Ajwad Creative/Getty Images

Printed in the United States of America

V10019161_061520

Contents

Introduction

Two friends used to go duck hunting together. Since they didn't have a bird-dog of their own, they went to the same location every year because they were able to rent a dog from the person who owned the property. After a while they found a dog that gave them particularly good results, so they requested him every time. They discovered the dog's name was Salesman and they used him for the next few years. On one of their annual trips, they asked for Salesman and found out that he wasn't available. They went to the owner and asked, "What happened to Salesman?" The owner replied, "You don't want to use him anymore because he got promoted to sales manager. The only thing he does now is lay around the office and bark at everyone."

Why We Wrote This Book

You've got this book in your hand, and you may be asking yourself, why did these guys write this book? We wrote this book because it takes a lot more than a barking sales manager to improve the performance of your sales team.

We wrote this book because we believe…

- Sales managers are pivotal. Sustained development of a sales team rides on the shoulders of the sales management team.

1

- Selling is a noble profession and we want to help the people who do it. Salespeople help buyers navigate purchase decisions, around the world, every minute, every day.
- It's important to share what we know best-in-class sales managers do with those who aspire to improve. Winning is fun! Helping others win even more so.
- An ineffective sales manager can have a neutral impact or negative impact because they fail to help their sales team grow out of their comfort zones and develop the habits and disciplines that generate success.
- An effective sales manager can have a dramatic impact on a salesperson's career and life. They help their sales team grow their skill set and develop the discipline, rigor, and proper habits to ultimately maximize their potential.
- Sales managers need to know how their team perceives the support they receive from them. According to Gallup, the best way to determine if you have a high-development culture is to ask your team to what degree they agree with the statement: "There is someone at work who encourages my development" (Clifton and Harter 2019, 6).

You deserve a practical playbook. It would be awesome if you worked for the greatest sales manager in the world, who could foster your development by setting a great example every day. Unfortunately, most of us don't have that. That's why we think sales managers deserve a practical playbook. We've been fortunate to code the DNA of what great sales managers do and we're going to share it with you.

Sales enablement technology can empower coaching, but sales managers must still possess the right attitudes and perform the right activities consistently to develop their team. While sales enablement technologies continue to evolve and get more powerful (for example, analytics, artificial intelligence, machine learning) it still, always, boils down to how well a sales manager coaches their sales team.

Who This Book is For

This book is for people who possess the right mindset, are motivated, want to get better, and want to help others get better.

Enterprise Rent-a-Car is one of the most successful car rental companies in the world, and one of the best sales organizations we've ever worked with. One of the keys to their success is that they have a very dynamic approach to sales coaching with the goal of growing the company while, at the same time, delivering great customer service. They believe their major priority is to develop their people. When they develop their people, they become more competitive and gain market share. Therefore, everyone in the company is genuinely invested in developing their people. If you have that sort of mindset, this book is for you.

In terms of job function, our intended audience includes:

- Senior sales executives.
- Line managers in sales and customer service.
- Aspiring sales or customer service managers.
- Contact center managers, leads, coaches, and quality assurance managers.
- Customer experience executives.
- Customer loyalty executives.
- Small business owners.
- Anyone in a leadership position at a law/accounting/consulting firm.

Who We Are

We have been successful salespeople, sales managers, business owners, and consultants. We started The Next Level Sales Consulting because, by working with other sales organizations, we found we could have a bigger impact, gain more experience and exposure, and (honestly) make more money. Together, we have over 50 years' experience in the trenches, training and coaching salespeople, sales managers, and sales executives.

Representative Client List

In addition to our own experience, we've been fortunate because we have partnered with some of the best sales organizations in America (and beyond) on sales force effectiveness projects that have helped them to better develop their sales leadership team and enjoy all the benefits that cascade from that. In this "laboratory of human experience," we have learned the best practices of top-performing companies and sales leaders, enabling us to repeat, refine, and innovate processes over time.

We probably benefited more from the relationships than they did. Hopefully we added value along the way. Thanks to all our valued clients, including:

American Express	MetLife
AT&T	Microsoft
Baird	Morgan Stanley Wealth Management
Bank of America	
Blue Cross Blue Shield	Raymond James
DIRECTV	RBC Wealth Management
Enterprise Rent-a-Car	Synchrony
Google	UBS Financial Services
ManpowerGroup	US Bank
Merrill Lynch Wealth Management	Wells Fargo Advisors
	Zurich Insurance

Triple-Distilled Sales Coaching Model

If you should ever have the opportunity to visit the Jameson Whiskey distillery in Dublin, Ireland, you will discover that Jameson Whiskey is triple distilled. The whiskey is purified, refined, and improved. Through that process they have developed a great-tasting whiskey – especially if you are a whiskey drinker. We have gone through a similar process to develop this book. We have worked with some of the best sales organizations in the country, gathered the best practices of their best sales

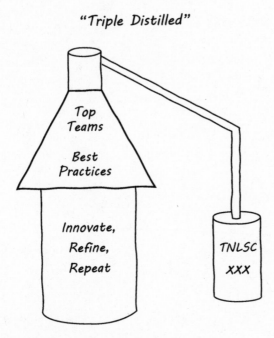

"Triple Distilled"

Top
Teams

Best
Practices

Innovate,
Refine,
Repeat

TNLSC
XXX

Figure I.1   Triple-Distilled Best Practices

leaders, distilled what we have learned, and refined it to make it better. Think of this book as the "triple-distilled" sales coaching process and methodology.

1

The Case for Sales Coaching

IN OVER 50 YEARS' combined experience training and coaching sales-people and their sales managers, we find that many of our clients share the same goals: to increase market share, revenue, and profitability.

Market share improves when sales performance improves. Sales performance improves when sales teams are better trained and coached, because it creates a cycle in which salespeople feel better about themselves and their career, experience more success, stay longer, and achieve even higher levels of success.

"Of all the codes Gallup has been asked to crack dating back 80 years to our founder, George Gallup, the single most profound, distinct and clarifying finding – ever – is probably this one: 70% of the variance in team engagement is determined solely by the manager" (Clifton and Harter 2019, 12).

Employee engagement drives retention, higher levels of buyer engagement, revenue, share price, and market share. The Gallup research validates everything we have learned over many years of helping companies improve the performance of their sales teams. Sales managers matter, you matter, and you can make a big difference!

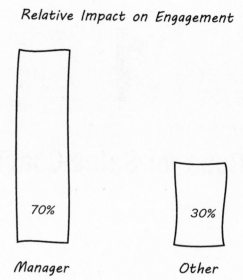

Figure 1.1   Relative Impact on Engagement

Dynamic Sales Coaching is Better than Random Sales Coaching

While implementing sales coaching programs for our clients' sales leadership teams, it is not uncommon for them to express very early in the process, "We're different. We are unique. We are not like everyone else."

You know what? They're right! We know that different companies take different approaches to sales coaching. Miller Heiman's CSO Insights 2019 Sales Enablement Report identified four different approaches (Miller Heiman 2019a, 34).

1. Random: 42.9% of companies take a random approach, in which sales coaching is completely left up to sales managers.
2. Informal: 20.0% take an informal approach, in which there may be guidelines.
3. Formal: 24.5% implement a formal approach.
4. Dynamic: 12.6% are dynamic, meaning that they have a formal sales coaching process and methodology, and enablement services tailored to individual salespeople.

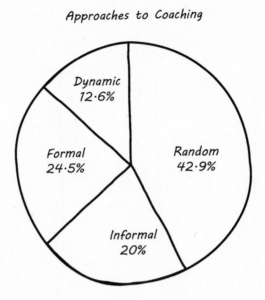

Approaches to Coaching

Dynamic 12·6%

Formal 24·5%

Random 42·9%

Informal 20%

Figure 1.2   Approaches to Coaching

Take a moment to reflect on your own experience. Does your company have a formal approach where there is a clearly defined sales coaching process and methodology that you have been trained on? Does your company take an informal approach in which there may or may not be guidelines? Or is it more random? We know there is a high probability that your company takes a random approach in which the sales coaching process and method is left entirely up to you.

Let's take a look at how sales coaching impacts win rates. Generally speaking, you don't get half a sale. You either get it, and you entered "closed-won" on your pipeline tracker, or you entered "closed-lost." It's all about the win rate.

So, what impact does the approach to sales coaching have on win rates?

- Companies with a *random* approach to sales coaching have a win rate of 41.8%.
- Companies with an *informal* approach have a win rate of 47.8%.
- Companies with a *formal* approach have a win rate of 48.9%.
- Companies with *dynamic* approach have a win rate of 55.2%.

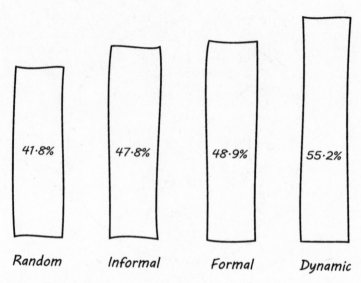

Figure 1.3 Coaching Approach and Win Rates

Dynamic sales coaching showed double-digit improvements in sales performance on both quota attainment (21.3%) and win rates (19.0%) over the study's average (Miller Heiman 2019a, 36).

What is the delta between random and dynamic? The dynamic approach outperforms the random approach by 32.1%. All the data from CSO Insights and Gallup are consistent with our own experience working with many large sales organizations on sales performance improvement programs.

In summary, we wrote this book to help you impact the level of engagement of your sales team, reduce the randomness in your sales coaching, increase the formality, and move you closer to a dynamic sales coaching process and methodology that will ultimately help you to win.

Winning isn't everything. It's the only thing.

—Vince Lombardi

The Benefits of Reading (and Using!) This Book

If you're like us, whenever you consider investing your most precious resource – your time – in reading a book, you are probably asking yourself: "What's in it for me? This book better be worth it!" We realize that, as a sales manager coaching your team, there are many challenges you are going to face. Here are just a few ...

Delivering Consistent Sales Performance as a Sales Manager

Quota achievement has improved a bit in the last few years, but it remains an extremely challenging environment, with only 56.9% of salespeople making goal (Miller Heiman 2019a, 3).

Shortening the Time to Proficiency for New Hires

Even if you have a great new-hire sales training program, the results are still going to depend to a wide degree on the sales manager, who has to know, demonstrate, reinforce, and coach what was covered in the sales training.

Developing the Untapped Potential of Your Sales Team

Many companies categorize their salespeople into "A," "B," and "C" players. "A" and "C" players together often compose about 10–15% of a typical sales force, while "B" players make up about 70–80%. Coaching will more effectively optimize the productivity of your "A" players. For "C" players, it will either "*help* them out," or it will "help them *out*." That's not a bad thing. Sometimes there are people in a sales role who are not a good fit for that role and it may be in their best interest to get on a path that might be more suitable for their skill set. The biggest opportunity is with the moveable middle, the "B" players. If you can incrementally improve the performance of the largest segment in your sales force, you can have a dramatic impact on the bottom line.

Developing Your Sales Team Through the Phases of Building a Business and Career

We find that many of our clients share similar goals when it comes to hiring, onboarding, training, coaching, and retaining talent. In that continuum, the first goal they have is to make sure people can survive and make it. After they have had success, the focus shifts to productivity. The best companies will then leverage those productive salespeople to be peer-to-peer coaches, ultimately grooming them to become future sales leaders. Teams that develop their sales leaders in this way are better positioned to be more competitive and gain market share.

Stays longer, sells more, succeeds, and coaches others...

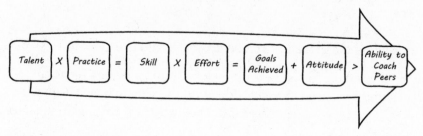

Figure 1.4   Stay Longer

Increasing Retention

Turnover in sales has increased to 18% (Miller Heiman 2019a, 4). The impact of this attrition includes the opportunity cost of having a territory/market vacant, plus the time it takes to source a new salesperson to move into the open role, compounded by the time it takes to get them to a desired level of productivity. Effective sales managers, in contrast, have a higher retention rate. They have more experienced, more productive, salespeople in the field longer, resulting in higher customer loyalty. They spend less time sourcing and onboarding new hires and more time coaching their sales team.

Leading a Diverse Workforce

This is the most diverse workforce in history. Millennials and Gen Zs typically like and expect ongoing feedback, positive reinforcement, and coaching to their strengths. You know what? So does everyone else! Even Boomers! We know more about the science of leadership today than we ever have. Leadership style and work environment affect our brains, our physiology, our culture, and our success (Pink 2009). Effective sales managers today must be able to communicate consistently and effectively while flexing their style, so they can be the coach that each unique salesperson needs.

Getting Competitive Results on "Great Place to Work" Surveys to Help Attract and Retain Talent

Your reputation as a workplace will determine the prospective talent you attract or repel. Your reputation lives in social media (and society generally), but it can be measured using employee engagement assessments. Using the sales coaching process and techniques in this book will help boost your scores in areas such as:

- I feel my work is recognized.
- Feedback is timely and consistent.
- My sales manager supports me.
- I know what my sales manager expects of me.
- I feel supported to pursue opportunities and grow.

Delivering Competitive Customer Satisfaction and "Net Promoter" Scores as a Customer Service Manager

The Net Promoter score is an index measuring the willingness of customers to recommend a company's products or services to others. It is used to measure the customer's overall satisfaction with a company's products or services and the customer's loyalty to the brand. Although the performance metrics may be different compared to sales teams, all the techniques in this playbook are applicable to a customer service environment where the Net Promoter score is an indication or reflection of the customer experience.

The questions we asked earlier were, "What's in it for me? Is it worth my time?" If you are facing any of these challenges, we think the juice will be worth the squeeze. We believe that the time you invest in reading this book will be well worth it. The fact of the matter is, if all you get out of this book is one good idea, it will be worth it.

What's in This Book

We believe in simplicity. This book is simple to use and easy to follow. It includes:

- A practical game plan you can start to use immediately.
- Easy to understand graphics for reference and sharing.
- Proven best practices from top-performing sales managers.
- Tools and templates.
- Inspiring quotes to get you motivated.
- Takeaway questions for individual reflection and team discussion.

What's NOT in This Book

This book is not designed to cover every area of responsibility a sales manager has. For example, we will not address hiring, recruiting, human resources issues, or compensation. We are purely focused on the sales coaching elements of the sales management role, because it has the biggest impact on performance.

Your Own Motivation, Drive, and Desire

We can show you what great sales managers do. But we can't do it for you. Only you can act on the principles in this book, and the drive to do that will come from within. What is not in this book is the motivation and desire to get better at coaching, be consistent, and adapt the tools to your specific situation. However, if you apply this coaching process consistently, you will increase your motivation, drive, and desire as you experience success.

It's kind of like diet books. There are thousands of them out there, and every year they publish more. A lot of people are looking for a book that will just promise them they can continue doing what they are now but get better results. In contrast, some people are so motivated they could read the world's shortest diet "book" (*Burn More Calories than You Consume*) and get amazing results. What kind of book are you looking for? If you're not that motivated, but you've already bought the book, or someone gave it to you, look on the bright side: you can always re-gift it or sell it on Amazon!

A Sales Process and Methodology

Another thing you won't find in this book – but will need – is a well-defined sales process and methodology as the framework for your coaching.

Just as with coaching, there are different organizational approaches to sales process and methodology. Some companies have a random approach, some informal, some formal, and some dynamic. In our experience, the most successful sales teams have a dynamic approach to selling, meaning it is formal and consistent, yet also adaptive to the individuals involved.

Are You Ready?

Are you ready for this book? Hopefully you answered "Yes!" because now is the time, you are the person, and this is the playbook. The largest room in the world is the room for improvement. You know you're ready if you:

- Believe you can make improvements to your sales coaching.
- Are open-minded to new ideas.
- Are not afraid to let your team know you are making changes for everyone's benefit.
- Are willing to live with some temporary discomfort while you and your team adopt and adapt to new tools and activities.
- Want to implement repeatable sales coaching and management processes that deliver predictable results.

Takeaway Questions

Below are questions you can use for further reflection.

Takeaway Discussion Questions for Your Organization

If you are leading a sales organization, here are some things to think about:

- Do you have a consistent sales process and methodology that is supported from the top down? If not, what can you do to promote one?
- How proficient are the sales managers on the sales process?
- How well-calibrated are they with one another on the sales process?
- How proficient and consistent are they on coaching and re-inforcing the sales process?
- To what degree are they open-minded to making changes?
- How open are they to new ideas that could potentially help them to become more effective managers?

Takeaway Questions for Personal Reflection

If you are leading a sales team, here are some things to think about:

- How open are you to new ideas?
- Do you believe you can make improvements to your sales coaching?
- Are you willing to let your team know you are making changes for everyone's benefit?
- Are you willing to live with some temporary discomfort while you and your team adopt and adapt to new tools and tips?
- Do you want to implement repeatable sales coaching and management processes that deliver predictable results? Why now?

The Road Ahead

In Chapter 2 we will look at the reasons that coaching fails, or fails to happen, by considering four sales manager personas: the Achiever, the Culture-Shocked, the Change Agent, and the Sales Rookie.

Chapter 3 introduces the critical sales management activities and attitudes, along with a self-assessment.

In Chapter 4 we cover (annual or semi-annual) review and plan meetings, including: key performance indicators, benefits of review and plan meetings for sales managers and salespeople, and the agenda for a review and plan meeting.

Goal-setting meetings provide the opportunity to follow up consistently on the goals set forth in the review and plan meeting, and we cover this in Chapter 5, including positive recognition, review of key performance indicators, skill development training, and building action plans.

In Chapter 6 we note the similarities between athletic performance and sales performance by talking about the importance of skill development training, and how to do it.

Check-ins are important to help salespeople sustain momentum, and we address this in Chapter 7.

In Chapter 8 we tackle live performance observation and feedback, including a discussion of co-selling roles and how to use live sales calls as opportunities to conduct skill development training.

Chapter 10 investigates team huddles, why they are important, and how they work, so you can inspire your team to great performance.

In Chapter 11 we provide seven best practices for coaching sales or service in the contact center, including tools you can use to build your team's skills, one at a time.

Chapter 12 discusses how to deploy sales enablement tools to enhance your sales coaching.

Finally, the Appendix includes examples of sales coaching cadences for field sales teams, inside sales teams, and contact center teams.

2

Why Coaching Fails or Fails to Happen

THE FOOTBALL TEAM was getting clobbered. The first-string quarterback was injured. The second-string quarterback was injured. Even the punter was injured. All the coach had left was the third-string quarterback who had yet to play a down all year. He pulled the quarterback aside. "Look, we can't afford to let them score again. We've got to run some time off the clock. Here's what I want you to do. On first down, run it to the left. On second down, run it to the right. On third down, run it up the middle. Then, on fourth down, punt it as far as you can punt it."

"OK coach!" said the quarterback. On first down, he ran it to the left for 30 yards. On second down, he ran it to the right for 40 more. On third down, he ran it up the middle to the one-yard line. Then, on fourth down, the quarterback dropped back and punted the ball right out of the end zone. When he got to the sideline, the coach was screaming, "What were you thinking?!!!?!!!" The quarterback replied, "I was thinking I must be playing for the dumbest coach in the world."

In this anecdote, the coach was not very effective. He gave the quarterback the plays to run but failed to make adjustments along the way. His prior experiences probably shaped what he felt the third-string quarterback was capable of and, therefore, underestimated his chances of success.

Personal Background

One of the reasons sales managers fail to coach, or fail at coaching, is because they've never been shown how to do it. Whether you are already in a sales management role, moving into a new sales management role, or considering doing so, you may find one or more of these profiles sounds familiar.

The Achiever

The salesperson who got promoted to sales manager, which is very common, and that could be you. You were a top-performing salesperson with a track record of success. You didn't need a lot of feedback, coaching, or support, so they just let you do your thing. You've done some peer-to-peer coaching and spoken at corporate events where you shared with the rest of the organization some of the things you've done to be successful. Based on your track record, you have been approached multiple times by sales leadership to consider moving into sales management. Finally, you decided to take the plunge. You haven't had any training on sales coaching, but you're a good salesperson. Because you don't have sales coaching skills, you revert to what you do best, which is selling. So, you find yourself going on sales calls to make sure deals get closed, but you're not really developing your team – and you know it. In fact, you get impatient trying to understand why your team does not seem to want to put in the hard work to improve.

The Culture-Shocked

The experienced sales manager who moved from one firm to another within the same industry and found it was a higher-performing culture. It's a big change because the culture is completely different. Your prior employer ran from the bottom up and your new one from the top down.

At your prior company, the tail wagged the dog. At the new company, the dog wags the tail. Your prior company did not offer much sales leadership training and now you are painfully aware that you don't have a defined sales coaching process for developing your team. You feel like you are in over your head, you've got a lot to learn, and you suspect the things you did to be successful in your former role may not get the same result in the new one. You now realize you need a plan, or you are going to be exposed.

The Change Agent

You came from a high-performance environment where there was a well-established sales process and methodology, as well as a sales coaching process and methodology. You had good training on both. Your new company is losing market share and wants to make changes but doesn't really have the sales culture required to do what they want to do. You were brought in as a change agent, but you realize you must be patient and adaptable and meet people where they are, because they are not the same caliber as the prior company. You know that in your new role you will be spending much more of your time than you did in the past developing the fundamental skills of your team. And you know you need to shift gears and adapt to your new environment.

The Sales Rookie

You were an experienced manager with no sales experience who transitioned into a sales management role within the company. You've been successful as a quality assurance manager in a large customer contact center. You have a lot of experience in call center operations, monitoring calls, and delivering quality assurance feedback, but the sales aspect was not part of the quality process. Now that you are a sales manager with a team of 12 agents dialing outbound for leads, you fear you lack credibility as a coach because you've never done the job.

These profiles don't exhaust all the scenarios, but they reveal the variables when someone is moving into a new sales management role. If one or more of the **risk factors** below apply to you, you will be among those who will benefit most from using this playbook:

- Moving from an individual contributor role as a salesperson into a sales management role.
- Moving from a non-sales management role to a sales management role.
- Changing industries.
- Moving up from a lower-performing culture to a higher-performing culture.
- Moving down from a higher-performing culture to a lower-performing culture.

Often, the flipside of risk is opportunity. Whatever your scenario, putting this playbook to work will give you a game plan you can execute from day one. You can invest all your energy and enthusiasm in doing the work, rather than wondering what to do.

Company Culture

In our experience, the quality and consistency of sales coaching among sales managers is akin to prospecting activity among salespeople. In other words, it's inconsistent. Spotty. All over the board. How about your company? Ask yourself if you agree or disagree with the statement: "Our sales managers effectively coach salespeople to higher levels of performance."

If you can't agree, with a straight face, you're not alone! According to Miller Heiman CSO Insights, only 33% of all companies agree vs. 90% of world-class sales organizations.

"What continues to raise eyebrows is the lack of effective sales coaching in sales organizations in spite of its well-known benefits" (Miller Heiman 2019b, 16).

What goes into "effective sales coaching"? We break it down into two components: quantity and quality.

Quantity: Why Managers Don't Coach Enough

Managers don't coach – or don't coach enough – when:

- They don't have an effective sales process to base their coaching on.
- Senior management doesn't support it – it's not part of the culture.
- They are effective at sales coaching, but don't prioritize it.
- They want to prioritize it, but don't know how to do it.
- They are unwilling to put in the time and effort.
- They spend a large portion of their time on administration and meetings.
- They mean well but don't have a well-established cadence of coaching activities.
- They lack credibility with their team due to lack of consistency and follow-up.
- Like fitness, it takes time, patience, and persistence to achieve positive results in terms of performance metrics.
- The sales manager fears the team won't be receptive to skills development training.

Which of these applies to you and/or your managers?

Quality: Why Sales Managers Coach Ineffectively

Sales managers fail at coaching when:

- They don't have an effective sales process to base their coaching on.
- They were formerly a top-performing salesperson, but sales coaching requires a different mindset and a different skill set.
- They don't know how to coach because they never had a good example to follow.
- They don't know how to "provide correction without stirring resentment" (UCLA basketball coach John Wooden). Their style puts their sales team on the defensive.
- They do it inconsistently, so they never get really good at it.

Most high-achieving salespeople are successful in sales because they have the type of self-esteem or makeup as a person that enables them to handle rejection, overcome fear, and have the confidence and resilience to handle the challenges sales presents. The really good ones do it in a world-class way. The one thing that helps them succeed in sales is possessing the emotional intelligence that enables them to succeed with all the obstacles and hurdles that come with the job. Conversely, when you become a sales manager, you will spend less time and effort on selling and more time and effort on training and coaching others. This is a big shift.

Before you are a leader, success is all about growing yourself. When you become a leader, success is all about growing others.

—Jack Welch

Takeaway Questions

Below are questions you can use for further reflection.

Takeaway Discussion Questions for Your Organization

- If you are leading a sales organization, does sales coaching fail/fail to happen?
- If yes, why?
- If no, what is the opportunity for improvement?

Takeaway Questions for Personal Reflection

- If you are leading a sales team, does sales coaching fail/fail to happen?
- If yes, why?
- If no, what is the opportunity for improvement?

3

Sales Coaching Model and Self-Assessment

WHAT MOST SALESPEOPLE want is a great job. That means they are engaged in meaningful work and they feel like they can grow and develop in their career. How salespeople feel about their job can affect other areas of their life too, such as their health and wellbeing. The problem is that not everybody feels like they have the greatest job in the world. One of the biggest determinants of how salespeople feel about their job is their sales manager. A sales manager can make a big difference in a salesperson's professional and personal life. Sales managers who have the ability to make a difference possess competencies that can be broken down into two essentials: the coaching activities they do and the attitudes they have when they do them.

Sales Coaching Model

Below are some of the essential sales coaching activities of successful sales managers.

- **Review and plan meetings.** You conduct review and plan conversations at regular intervals (e.g. annually or bi-annually) to establish

Sales Coaching Model

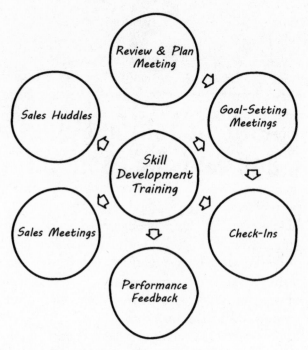

Figure 3.1   Sales Coaching Model

metrics for both results and the activities that will generate the results.

- **Goal-setting meetings.** You consistently (for example, bi-weekly or monthly) review performance results and update goals for your sales team's results.
- **Check-ins.** You check in either formally or informally. Your team knows that you will be checking in to see how it is going, what's working and what's not working, and what progress they are making toward achieving their goals.
- **Skill development training.** You know your sales process and methodology and have the ability to train and coach those skills efficiently and effectively. You proactively create opportunities to

conduct skill development training to reinforce the sales process with your team.

- **Performance feedback.** You consistently spend time in the field or on the phone, observing your sales team and providing feedback, or, when you are selling together (co-selling and you are in the role of the leader), you demonstrate the sales process and methodology at a high level; you provide opportunities for skill development training between calls or meetings based on your observations.
- **Sales meetings.** You consistently hold inspirational meetings (weekly, bi-weekly, or monthly) that include opportunities for skill development training, sharing success stories and best practices, goal reporting and goal setting, and recognition.
- **Sales huddles.** You hold brief huddles for your sales team that are motivating, informative, and provide opportunities for skill development training, recognition, performance results, and key focus areas for the day. You provide on-the-job development activities so your team can further develop their selling skills.

Sales Manager Attitudes

Here are the attitudes we believe are essential for sales managers:

- **Enthusiasm.** You are enthusiastic and open to being coached yourself. You are optimistic that your team can improve. *You need a spark to light a fire. Nothing works better than the spark of enthusiasm.*
- **Communication.** You say what you mean and mean what you say. Your sales team regards you as a good listener who seeks first to understand. You are effective with the Socratic method – using questions to stimulate thinking and draw out ideas, helping your sales team come to their own conclusions rather than you lecturing them. Most salespeople don't want to get whipped into a nap by a lecture from their sales manager that could put a container of NoDoze® to sleep.

tability. Your salespeople are motivated by different things and learn in different ways. You flex your sales coaching to meet the needs of unique individuals.

- **Patience.** You realize that everyone learns and implements things at different paces. The rest of this book could be written on all the different situations you will encounter as a sales manager where patience is required, but it's not. That's for another book.
- **Persistence.** As with fitness training, you persist in doing the right things consistently over time, knowing it will pay off over the long haul. You overcome resistance and fatigue because you care about your sales team and you have your eyes on the goal. You have to have the mindset that, as you persist with your sales coaching, you are not doing it *to* them, you are doing it *for* them. You have their best interests at heart and have your eye on the long-term objective. Persistence overcomes resistance.

Figure 3.2   Sales Manager Attitudes

Sales Manager Self-Assessment: Attitudes and Activities

Use the activities and attitudes below to complete a self-assessment of your sales coaching readiness. Score yourself on both quantity/consistency and quality/skill for each of the coaching activities listed in Table 3.1. Quantity/consistency refers to frequency and the timeliness of the coaching activity, while quality and skill are how effectively you're doing it.

Table 3.1

Activity	Quantity/Consistency	Quality/Skill
Review and plan		
Goal-setting meetings		
Skill development training		
Check-ins		
Performance feedback		
Skill development training		
Sales meetings		
Sales huddles		

Table 3.2

Attitude
Enthusiasm
Communication
Adaptability
Patience
Persistence

In Table 3.2, rate yourself on a 1-to-5 scale on sales coaching attitudes: 1 = poor; 2 = fair; 3 = good; 4 = very good; 5 = excellent.

Impact of Coaching

Why should you make the investment to improve your sales coaching? Because it will help you to:

- Have a positive personal and professional impact on your sales team members.
- Enhance the culture of your sales team.
- Develop your salespeople to win more opportunities in the marketplace.

- Have a lasting effect on your "A," "B," and "C" players. Higher achievers get better faster, the middle improves faster, and poor performers are able to move on to the next opportunity.
- Increase loyalty and retention, which drives tenure and experience, which produce results.
- Build a bench of future leaders.
- Improve revenue.
- Gain market share.

Takeaway Questions

Below are questions you can use for further reflection.

Takeaway Discussion Questions for Your Organization

- If you are leading a sales organization, based on this sales coaching self-assessment on attitudes and activities, what do you think are your sales leaders' strengths?
- What are their opportunities for improvement?

Takeaway Questions for Personal Reflection

- If you are leading a sales team, based on your sales coaching self-assessment on attitudes and activities, what are your strengths?
- What are your opportunities for improvement?

4

Review and Plan Meetings

Review & Plan Meeting

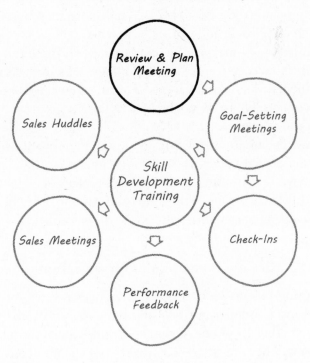

Plans are nothing; planning is everything.
—Dwight D. Eisenhower

GREAT COACHES AT both the collegiate and professional levels are able to replicate their success over time because they have repeatable processes that work. One is their ability to develop relationships with their team and a second is their ability to plan. We are going to reach now and draw some conclusions. At the beginning of each season, they meet with each individual player and review what happened last year and set goals for the upcoming year. In sales management terminology, we would call this conversation a "review and plan." Throughout the course of the season they continue having these conversations to ensure progress against the goals and make adjustments when necessary. Before, during, and after games, they have impactful meetings and huddles to get everyone motivated and focused to hit the goal, which is to win the game.

They run practices and trust that repetition will help develop individual player skills, team skills, and the ability to perform under pressure. During games they shoot video. At half-time, they review it, break it down, give feedback, and make adjustments.

It takes a lot of time, persistence, patience, and attention to detail to be a successful coach, and that is what most sales managers are able, but unwilling, to do. At times, it can be much easier to hide in activities that are comfortable to do yet have very little impact on the performance of the sales team.

In most organizations there is a year-end performance review but that is not enough. Perhaps the single most important skill a sales manager can have is translating goals into action plans on a daily, weekly, and monthly basis, because if the sales team is doing the right activities the greatest percentage of the time goals will be achieved.

Planning Varies by Type of Sales Organization

The planning process looks a little different depending on context. Field and inside sales teams typically have to go out and find new business, whether by phone, foot, networking, social media, or some other means. They are trying to convert contacts into conversations,

conversations into leads, and leads into sales. They may have a monthly and annual quota; or they may be building their own book of business according to their own business plan. One topic that gets a lot of airtime in review and plan meetings is key performance indicators (KPIs).

A KPI is a measurable value that demonstrates how effectively a salesperson, sales team, or company is achieving important business objectives. Organizations use KPIs to evaluate their success in reaching their goals. In a sales organization there could be an inside sales team, an outside sales team, or a customer service team. Each one of these teams could have a different set of KPIs to measure success based on the goals and targets they want to achieve. Example KPIs for an outside sales team include:

- contacts
- lead generation
- appointments set and held
- sales conversion
- pipeline management
- territory management
- quota achievement
- personal business planning

Contact center sales and service teams may be large or small, but typically have a sales manager-to-salesperson ratio of about 1:10–12. The environment allows for ongoing observation, measurement, and feedback, as well as frequent team huddles. Example KPIs for this type of sales team include:

- calls per day or total on-phone time
- handle time per call
- lead generation (outbound)
- sales conversion (inbound or outbound)
- customer retention rate (inbound)
- customer satisfaction

A large part of the planning process is the establishment of KPIs and the conversations that happen throughout the year about the progress made toward the achievement of KPIs.

Benefits of Review and Plan Conversations

Regardless of the type of sales team you work on, a formal planning meeting should be held when a new hire is onboarded. Then, a review and plan meeting should be held – at minimum – annually or bi-annually thereafter. So, what are some of the benefits of review and plan meetings for sales managers?

A consistent process of review and plan conversations is beneficial because:

- It gives you a chance to rise above all the noise and distractions, candidly assess past performance, and imagine the future.
- It helps you avoid stress, knowing you have already prioritized activities and are executing proactively against that list.
- In the heat of the battle, it helps you stay focused on what is most important. Your proactive cadence of coaching activities will naturally address challenges, but also prevent them.
- It provides daily, weekly, monthly, and yearly criteria for whether your sales team is productive rather than just busy. There is a difference between motion and progress. If you have ever seen a rocking chair, you probably noticed that there is a lot of movement, but it doesn't go anywhere.

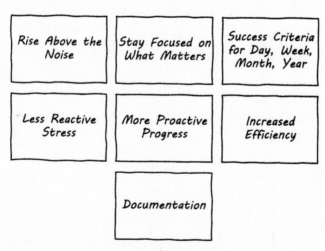

Figure 4.1   Review and Plan Manager Benefits

- You can be more efficient because you're focused on the activities that get the best results and don't have to think too much about what to do each day.
- You can more easily help move unproductive salespeople on to other opportunities because you have documentation of action plans, results, and feedback.

Salespeople benefit in numerous ways from review and plan meetings:

- The dialogue and review and plan process build the relationship. The sales manager can learn what motivates their sales team members and the team can clearly see their manager is invested in their success.
- It provides a reference point and context throughout the year for discussing, evaluating, and planning to improve performance.
- The sales manager can provide inspiration and encouragement because they know what motivates their salespeople.
- When the sales manager knows what the salesperson's plan is for the year, they are able to deliver performance feedback that is appropriate and relevant to how the salesperson is progressing throughout the year against their goals.

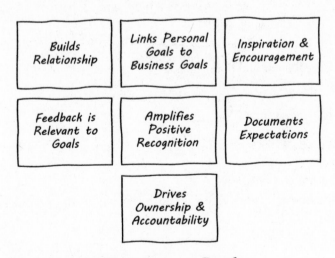

Figure 4.2   Review and Plan Salesperson Benefits

mplifies positive recognition because it measures accomplishment.

- It documents expectations.
- It helps drive ownership and accountability because it was developed collaboratively by both the sales manager and the salesperson.

Review and Plan Conversation

Review & Plan Meeting

- ✓ Celebrate last year's successes
- ✓ Career goals
- ✓ Sales goals for coming year
- ✓ Personal development goals
- ✓ Desired coaching and support

Figure 4.3   Review and Plan Agenda

Successes – Example Questions

- As you look back over last year, what were some of your biggest successes?
- What are you most proud of?
- What obstacles did you encounter and how did you overcome them?

Career Goals – Example Questions

- Why did you select a career here? What keeps you here?
- What are your career goals for the year?
- What are your long-term career goals?
- How do you feel you are using your strengths in your current role?
- What are some goals outside of work?
- How does what you do here support your goals outside of work?

Sales Goals – Example Questions

- What is your sales goal for this year?
- What is your new business development strategy for this year?
- What is your strategy for existing clients?
- Walk me through a typical day, week, and month of sales activity for you.
- What results are you expecting to accomplish weekly, monthly, quarterly, and yearly?
- What do you think will be the biggest challenge you will face this year in achieving your goals?

Personal Development Goals – Example Questions

- What personal development goals do you have?
- What knowledge and skills do you want to improve on to get to the next stage in your career?
- What are you planning to do to accomplish that?

Coaching and Support – Example Questions

- How do you learn best?
- What kind of coaching and support do you expect from me?
- What is the best way to give you feedback?

Confirm *Understanding*

Thanks for sharing that information with me. Let's review what we discussed to make sure I understand your situation:

- last year's successes
- career goals
- sales goals for the coming year
- goals for personal development
- desired coaching and support.

Have I missed anything?
Is there anything you would like to add?

Give Encouragement – Examples

- I believe you have a strong business strategy for hitting your weekly, monthly, and annual goals.
- I also have a good understanding of the things that motivate you, how you like to be coached, and what kind of support you expect from me this year.
- I am confident you can execute your plan and I promise to do everything I can to help you get there – are you ready?!

Review and Plan Meeting Tips

Over time, the annual performance review has come to be perceived as something it probably was not meant to be. It is a bigger conversation than compensation and future career aspirations. This conversation can be very powerful when focused on celebrating success, discussing goals and motivators, setting activity and metrics, objectives for the following year, and discussing preferred support the salesperson would like to receive from their sales manager.

The review and plan meeting could last from one to three hours. Make sure to plan the appropriate amount of time on the calendar to conduct the meeting effectively. Don't rush.

After each individual salesperson on the team has completed their plan and you have gone over it together in the review and plan meeting, have them present it to the rest of the sales team. This enables peer-to-peer idea sharing, drives accountability, and inspires competition.

Even though review and plan meetings are often conducted annually, they should be revisited periodically to ensure alignment and make adjustments. This ensures the plan remains relevant throughout the year and can be used to effectively measure activities and results.

Ensure that goals are realistic and reflect the market realities of the day. Salespeople will become demotivated if it becomes clear that they are given (or have set for themselves) goals that are unattainable due to factors outside their control.

Make sure to formally document the review and plan meeting by having the salesperson send a summary to the sales manager after the meeting for review and approval. Review the document throughout the year at appropriate intervals (for example, monthly or quarterly).

Takeaway Questions

Below are questions you can use for further reflection.

Takeaway Discussion Questions for Your Organization

If you are leading a sales organization, your sales management team probably conducts review and plan meetings already with their salespeople.

- What questions do they ask that are similar to or different from the example questions given?
- What is their opportunity for improvement?

Takeaway Questions for Personal Reflection

If you are leading a sales team, here are some things to think about:

(continued)

(*continued*)

- How have you conducted review and plan meetings in the past? How was it different from the process recommended?
- What can you do to improve your review and plan meetings?
- How can you leverage review and plan meetings throughout the year?

5

Goal-Setting Meetings

Goal-Setting Meetings

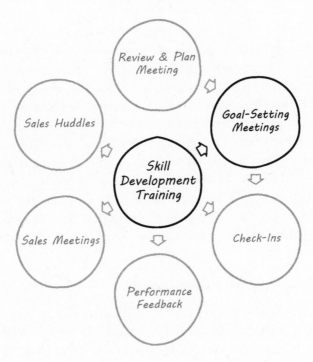

NOW THAT YOU HAVE had a review and plan meeting, one way to continue the conversation through the course of the year is to conduct goal-setting meetings. The purpose of these meetings is to check in on a consistent basis on the progress being made on the goals and objectives that were agreed to in the plan. The plan documents goals for the year. The goal-setting meeting takes the larger goal and breaks it down into smaller bite-size pieces to be accomplished in a shorter time frame. From our experience in working with our clients, we have found that goal-setting meetings are optimally conducted monthly or semi-monthly. They typically last 30 to 60 minutes. The duration of the meeting is in correlation to your salesperson's individual situation. These meetings are planned on the calendar and the conversation is based on successes, recognition, progress against action steps and key performance indicators (KPIs), and your salesperson's need for support from you.

> *The key to success is consistency.*
>
> —Zak Frazer

Consistent goal-setting meetings help you to build relationships by providing regular communication between you and your salespeople. They also provide opportunities for coaching and support, allowing you to resolve your sales team's concerns, and provide opportunities for your salespeople to make the connection between their own goals and the goals of the company. In addition, goal-setting meetings provide a means for exchanging information and solving problems. Consistency with goal-setting meetings helps you build and maintain credibility and trust with your team. The one thing you do not want to do is reschedule your team's goal-setting meetings around everything else, which is a common pitfall for sales managers. You want to schedule your goal-setting meetings and schedule other activities around them.

Why Salespeople Miss Expectations

Let's assume you have had the review and plan meeting with each member of your team at the start of the year. You will begin to follow up on the activities and execution of the plan on a frequent basis. When you do this, you will discover that some salespeople on your team are on or ahead of target, while others are off target. Some reasons salespeople fall short of expectations may be:

- They don't know or understand the priorities and expectations.
- They lack the required skills.
- They possess the skills, but lack the will, commitment, and work ethic.
- They lack the tools and resources to do the job.
- They believe the goals and expectations are unattainable.
- They are not receiving the type of coaching they need from their sales manager on a consistent basis to help them achieve their goals.

> *No one has ever drowned in sweat.*
>
> —Lou Holtz

In your experience, which of these six reasons have you encountered? These six reasons are exactly why you need to have consistent goal-setting meetings with every salesperson on your team. The reason why they are not hitting goals will manifest itself earlier in these conversations. You will be able to address any of these issues much earlier rather than later. To give you an analogy, as a sales manager, would you rather be a fire fighter or a fire preventer?

Guidelines for Conducting Goal-Setting Meetings

The goal-setting meeting conversation centers on a discussion of KPIs. KPIs are those performance areas that will move salespeople towards achieving their individual goals, as well as supporting the sales team's goals. Therefore, it is critical that you have regular communication with each salesperson about their performance in each KPI on a consistent basis.

The frequency and duration of goal-setting meetings varies depending on the type of sales organization and the salesperson's level of experience and effectiveness. For example, a call center sales team that has high call volume and short sales cycles might have weekly one-on-one goal-setting meetings lasting 30 minutes. Alternately, a field sales team might hold monthly one-on-one goal-setting meetings lasting 60 minutes. If a salesperson is less experienced or underperforming, you may want to increase the frequency. These meetings can be conducted face to face, or virtually. Goal-setting meetings should be:

- Of optimal frequency and duration for the sales team and the salesperson.
- Scheduled early enough in the reporting period (for example, the last week of the month or the first week of the month) to impact the results. When the meeting is in the middle of the month, your salespeople will probably ask themselves, "The month is already half over. Why are we doing this now?"
- Planned for and scheduled in advance.
- A top priority that seldom gets canceled or pushed, and only for an urgent and important matter that needs to be addressed immediately.
- Documented and retained for future reference.
- Responsive to a salesperson's individual needs and social style.
- Uninterrupted – no electronic devices (unless recording video of sales skills).

Goal-Setting Meeting Overview

Two things happen in a well-conducted goal-setting meeting. One is the high quality of the conversation and interaction between the sales manager and the salesperson. The second is how well that conversation gets documented. Because of this, we recommend you use a goal-setting meeting form that will help guide the conversation in the meeting and enable you to document it. Keep in mind that the most important thing in the goal-setting meeting is the conversation – you are only using the form to document the conversation. So, we are going to introduce you to a goal-setting meeting template that we have used with our clients as a starting point that you can customize to your sales team. We strongly recommend that you limit the goal-setting meeting form to one page.

Let's take a look at how you can use the template to help guide the flow of the conversation in the meeting.

Goal-Setting Meeting

Name   **Date**

Biggest Victory Since Last GSM

Action Steps from Last GSM	Completion %

Key Performance Indicators	Goal	Actual	(+/-)	Next Goal

Observations

Account Executive Action Steps for Next GSM	Date

Sales Manager Action Steps for Next GSM	Date

Next GSM Date: **Time:**

Account Executive Signature   **Sales Manager Signature**

Figure 5.1   Blank Goal-Setting Form

Goal-Setting Meeting Process

Step 1: Agenda
- Review biggest victory since last goal-setting meeting.
- Review last goal-setting meeting action steps.
- Review KPIs.
- Build action steps.
- Gain input on agenda from your salesperson.

Step 2: Discovery
- Biggest victory since last goal-setting meeting.
- Review action steps from last goal-setting meeting and completion status.
- Review KPI goals vs. actual performance. What's working/not working?
- Document observations.
- Confirm understanding.

Step 3: Action plan
- Define clear action steps for the salesperson.
- Define clear action steps for the sales manager.

Step 4: Summarize, gain commitment, and set next meeting
- Salesperson reviews their action steps.
- Sales manager reviews their action steps.
- Set date and time of next goal-setting meeting.

Step 5: Give encouragement
- Express your optimism.
- Be sincere and specific.

Step 1: Agenda

You will begin your goal-setting meetings with preliminary pleasantries to break the ice. You will then transition into setting an agenda to start the meeting on a positive note and establish a clear focus. This will help you to keep the meeting on track and cover all the important topics you want to cover in the time you have scheduled for the meeting.

Goal-Setting Meeting Agenda

✓ Discovery – KPIs & Observations

✓ Action Steps

✓ Summarize & Gain Commitment

✓ Give Encouragement

Figure 5.2   Agenda for a Goal-Setting Meeting

Sales manager: [Salesperson's name], I'm glad we have set aside this morning to work together. The purpose of our meeting is to come up with a plan to help you achieve your goals. In order to maximize our time, I suggest we follow this agenda:

- First, let's review your biggest victory that you are most proud of since our last meeting.
- Then, we can review how you did on your last set of action steps.
- After that, we can look at your goals (KPIs) since we last met to see how you did.
- Then, we can set new goals and come up with action steps and a plan to get you there.
- We can also discuss what you need from me next month to help you achieve your goals.

Is there anything you would like to add to the agenda [Salesperson's name]?

Great, then why don't we start by discussing your biggest victory since our last meeting...

Step 2: Discovery

Review the Biggest Victory Since the Last Goal-Setting Meeting
After you get permission (with a "Yes!") from your salesperson to move to discovery, start by reviewing their biggest victory since the last goal-setting meeting. When reviewing the biggest victory since the last goal-setting meeting, remember that the victory could be results-oriented, but it could also be behavior-oriented. In fact, it could be both.

> *The word LISTEN contains the same letters as SILENT.*
> —Alfred Bentel

A results-oriented victory is typically a byproduct of behaviors that created a positive outcome. You want to reward the behavior more than the outcome. That is why you want to ask the salesperson questions to determine what they did to achieve success. This is not just informational. When the salesperson verbalizes a response, they first have to reflect and crystallize their thinking about what they did and how they did it. In addition, the act of telling their story functions as an "active, public commitment" (Cialdini). They are more likely to repeat the positive behavior in the future because they now identify with it.

You will begin this part of the conversation by asking, "What was your biggest victory since we last met?" Then, you will want to drill down to gain further clarity about the behavior that created the victory.

Ask your salesperson questions, such as:

How did you accomplish that?

What did you do to make that happen?

What did you do different than last month?

What did you do more of?

What did you do less of?

What did you start doing?

What did you stop doing?

What did you do better?

While you are asking questions and listening, you will be taking notes in the box on the goal-setting meeting form: Biggest victory since last goal-setting meeting.

After you identify the behavior(s) that created the success, compliment your salesperson on the **behavior** as opposed to complimenting them on the achievement. You want to continue to maximize the strengths that your salespeople already have. A sales culture that supports recognizing strengths will help you attract and keep top talent. For example:

Sales manager: Charles, congratulations on your success in sending an agenda for each of your prospect meetings last month via email and asking your prospects if there is anything they would like to add to that agenda. Then, taking the feedback they gave you and updating your agenda and using the printed agenda in the actual meeting itself. Secondarily, great work on following up your prospect meetings within 24 hours with an executive summary that confirms what happened in the meeting and sets next steps. Keep doing what you're doing. It is working!

As a sales manager, when you encourage and reinforce a behavior that works, it is highly likely that your salesperson will be motivated and inspired to continue that behavior, especially if it leads to good on-the-job performance. The bottom line is that you get more of the behavior that you reward. Most salespeople like to receive positive

Goal-Setting Meeting

Name Mark Norman   **Date** 4/1

Biggest Victory Since Last GSM
Success starting every meeting with printed agenda. Prospects liked that I was prepared. Good feedback from sending Executive Summary within 24 hours of the meeting – actually landed a $300,000 opportunity!

Figure 5.3   Record the Biggest Victory

feedback and avoid doing things that generate negative feedback or no reward. Ultimately, rewarding positive behavior will help your salespeople to cultivate good habits and routines that create success over time.

When you start the goal-setting meeting with the biggest victory, you create a positive environment up-front, rather than beginning the meeting focused solely on numbers, your salesperson's weaknesses, attempts at correcting behaviors that may or may not be working, and with you doing all of the talking. This is not the way to begin a goal-setting meeting. It is a way to start a goal-setting beating.

> *A word of encouragement from a leader can inspire a person to reach their potential.*
>
> —John Maxwell

Review Action Steps from Last Goal-Setting Meeting and Completion Status   After you have covered the biggest victory, the next step in discovery is to ask questions that help you gain an understanding of how your salesperson did on their action steps and their level of execution on what they set out to do. In digging deeper on how well the salesperson carried out their action steps, it is a great opportunity to determine a skill, will, or attitude issue that may be limiting the salesperson from achieving their goals. It creates the opportunity to do three things:

1. Deliver positive feedback if they executed well on a specific action step.
2. Give constructive feedback on what they could potentially have done differently on the execution of their game plan.
3. Give corrective feedback if the behaviors that created specific results need to be changed.

We want to take you through the five-step process of how to conduct a goal-setting meeting first, because we feel it will be the best way for you to get the flow down. Later in the chapter, we will address how to deal with difficult attitude issues, whether in a goal-setting

Action Steps from Last GSM	Completion %
Attend 4 networking events > 3 contacts per	25%
Make 20 calls per day > 4 prospects > set 1 meeting	75%
Daily LinkedIn: 3 connection requests, 1 intro, 1 meeting	100%
Ask for referral at 4 recommendation meetings this month	100%

Figure 5.4   Review the Action Steps

meeting or a stand-alone conversation. Oftentimes, attitude issues can have far-reaching consequences that can impact more than just the salesperson's performance. It can impact you and other members of the sales team as well.

Reviewing action steps and completion status is the accountability loop that connects this meeting to the prior goal-setting meeting. You will begin this part of the conversation with a question like, "We put some action steps in place in the last meeting. How did they go?"

Define Action Steps   Before we can discuss reviewing action steps in the goal-setting meeting, we need to talk about the difference between quality action steps and poor action steps. Action steps need to be specific, so everyone knows exactly what is to be done by when. Action steps should follow the S.M.A.R.T. formula. They need to be specific, measurable, actionable, realistic, and within a given timeframe. Here are some examples of action steps. Which of these fit the S.M.A.R.T. formula?

I'm going to go to a bunch of networking events next month.

I'm going to hit the phones and make more calls.

I'm going to use LinkedIn.

I'm going to ask for more referrals.

You will notice that none of these action steps follow the formula. Because they do not, they will be very difficult to follow up on in the next goal-setting meeting. Here are some examples of action steps that fit the S.M.A.R.T. formula:

- Attend four networking events with a goal of making three new contacts per event.
- Make 50 calls per day with a goal of contacting four prospects to set one meeting.
- Use LinkedIn daily: send three connection requests, ask one connection for a meeting, ask one connection for an introduction.
- Ask for a referral at the end of each of my four recommendation meetings this month.

Review Action Steps   Make sure to have the action steps from the last goal-setting meeting already filled in at the top of the form. When reviewing action steps with your salespeople, stay away from closed-ended questions like, "Did you get your action steps completed?" Stick with open-ended questions like, "We had an action step of [fill in action step]. How did that go?" Going back to our example, it would sound like, "We had an action step of attending four networking events with a goal of getting three new contacts per event. How did that go?" You will then ask additional clarifying questions to gain a greater understanding of how things turned out with the execution of their action steps. Ask your salesperson questions such as:

What were the four networking events you planned to go to last month?

Why did you select those four events?

How many were you able to make it out to?

How did it go at the events you were able to make it out to?

Were you able to establish any meaningful contacts?

What follow-up did you do with the prospects you met after the event?

What prevented you from going to the other events?

While you are reviewing the action steps from the last goal-setting meeting, it is very important to document their level of execution on what they committed to. While you are doing this, there could be some discomfort when the salesperson is answering the questions around why they did not complete an action step, especially if the action step was doable. This could be a good thing. It may be a motivator for them to do a better job to complete their action steps in the future, because they don't want to have to have another conversation with you about why they are not getting it done. On the contrary, when they do accomplish their action steps, they can't wait to meet with you at the next goal-setting meeting to tell you how they got it done. Here is one way to document status:

- incomplete
- 25% complete
- 50% complete
- 75% complete
- 100% complete.

Documenting the status provides clarity on where the salesperson stands on the execution of their plan. It removes ambiguity from what actually happened. In addition to indicating the status, you will be documenting key points of the conversation in the observations box. For example, if a salesperson had an action step they were unable to achieve due to some unforeseen event, that should be documented on the form.

> *Accountability is the glue that ties commitment to the result.*
> —Bob Proctor

Review KPI Goals vs. Actual Performance What's working and what's not working? Now that you have discussed the action steps set in the last meeting as well as the completion status for each of those action steps, it is time to transition into a conversation focused on the KPIs. It is not uncommon for a sales manager to go right down the form, one KPI at a time, and peel the onion back on the outcome of each KPI. Confirm the current goal, the actual, over/under, and the goal for the next meeting. Here is a list of some example questions you could use when goals are achieved:

Congratulations. What enabled you to hit the goal?
What worked?

What did you start, stop, or keep doing to achieve success?

What did you learn?

Let's confirm the goals for each KPI for the next meeting.

When there is a shortfall in a salesperson's performance, you will want to ask specific questions to understand the underlying reason for the shortfall. With a high degree of probability, it will come down to a skill gap, a will issue, or their attitude. Once you diagnose the root cause of the shortfall, you will be able to address it in a variety of ways that we will cover later in the book. If it's a skill gap, you may close the gap with skill development training. If the cause for poor performance is a will issue, you can accelerate the frequency of your goal-setting meetings. For example, from monthly to bi-weekly, to weekly, to daily, to hourly. (Just kidding, daily might be too much – they will feel like they are working under a microscope.) If attitude contributed to the shortfall, you will ask them questions to encourage them to self-identify the attitude that is hindering their ability to achieve their goals. If, through that conversation, they are able to identify the attitude, you will ask them what they think they could start or stop doing to change the behavior and, thus, change their attitude. On the contrary, you may have observed an attitude they demonstrated through their behaviors that could be contributing to the shortfall. In this case, you may suggest or recommend what they could start or stop doing. Here is a list of some example questions:

Walk me through the shortfall.

What didn't work?

Key Performance Indicators	Goal	Actual	(+/-)	Next Goal
Contacts	80	60	-20	80
Connection meetings	20	15	-5	20
Discovery meetings	8	6	-2	8
Recommendation meetings	4	3	-1	4
New relationships opened	2	1	-1	2
Revenue	250,000	300,000	50,000	250,000

Figure 5.5   Reviewing KPIs

What obstacles did you encounter? What got in your way?

What did you learn from that experience?

Moving forward, what will you stop, start, or keep doing?

What is your goal between now and our next meeting?

While you are asking questions to gain more specificity of exactly what happened with your salesperson's performance since the last goal-setting meeting, you will be taking notes in the observations box on the form. Just like you are asking questions about the action steps and documenting observations, you will do the same thing with the KPIs.

The observations box provides a narrative of the dynamics that occurred between goal-setting meetings. This narrative will help you and your salesperson articulate what happened and why with clarity. Many sales managers report to executive leadership at the regional or divisional level, who like to have a window into how the sales manager's team is doing. It's very common for these sales executives to have a goal-setting meeting with their sales managers. If that applies to you, you can present your sales executives with the completed goal-setting meeting forms for your entire sales team. They should be able to read through the forms and have a meaningful conversation with you about what's happening with your sales team. In addition, if you get promoted and your replacement steps into your role, you can use the completed goal-setting meeting forms to help ease the transition for both your replacement and the sales team. The incoming sales manager can read through the past several months' goal-setting meeting forms for each member of the sales team and gain an understanding of each salesperson's performance over time.

Observations
Great job last month using meeting agendas and executive summaries. You made 1 networking event and 4 meaningful contacts but fell short of 4 events due to a lot of time on the large opportunity. Great job with your calls but came up a short of your contact goal due to extra time preparing the proposal. You were very consistent with LinkedIn activity in the morning every day. Nice work asking for referrals at your recommendation meetings. You got 2 introductions in your target market.

Figure 5.6   Record Observations

The key learning here is that, when you are conducting your goal-setting meetings, you want to document your conversations so that anyone reading the forms is able to gain a baseline understanding of each salesperson's performance over time.

Confirmation of Understanding

People want to be heard, not herded.

—Steve Johnson

After you document the conversation in the observations box, you will then reflect back to the salesperson what you believe you heard so you can confirm your understanding of their situation and they can verbally agree (Cialdini's principle of commitment). Here is an example outline of how the confirmation of understanding could flow.

Sales manager: [Salesperson's name], thanks for sharing that information with me. Let's review what we discussed to make sure I understand your situation. Let's:

- Highlight the biggest victory since last goal-setting meeting.
- Highlight last month's goal-setting meeting action steps and status.
- Highlight KPIs exceeded or fallen short and areas of improvement.
- Review your goals.

[Salesperson's name], let's review what we discussed to make sure I understand your situation. Great job last month. Particularly with using meeting agendas and executive summaries to prepare for and summarize meetings. You were able to make it out to one networking event and made four meaningful contacts but fell short of getting to all four events because you spent a lot of time bringing in the large opportunity that you closed. You did a great job with your calls but came up a little short of your contact goal due to the extra time you spent preparing the proposal for your big deal. You were very consistent with your LinkedIn activity. You did it first thing in the morning, every morning with your first cup of coffee. Nice work asking for referrals at the end of your recommendation meetings. You got two quality introductions that are in your target market. You'd like to keep the same set of goals that you had last month.

Have I missed anything?

Now let's put together some action steps moving forward that will help you to reach your goals.

Why is the confirmation of understanding so impactful?

- It shows your salesperson that you care.
- It tells them that you heard, listened, and attempted to understand them.
- If your confirmation of understanding is accurate, it allows you both to gain agreement on what happened.
- It provides an opportunity for further clarification.
- It deepens trust in the relationship.

Step 3: Action Plan

Once you have asked questions, listened, taken notes, and reflected back a confirmation of understanding, it is time to transition into setting action steps. Ideally, you will coach your salesperson to help them develop the action steps they are ultimately going to execute. This is done by asking focused questions and believing that salespeople have the ability to solve their own problems, overcome obstacles, and hit their goals. There are two styles that can be utilized to develop action steps – telling and asking.

Telling vs. Asking Styles for Developing Action Plans Using a telling strategy, you will do more of the talking and be more involved in communicating to the salesperson exactly what the action steps should look like. This approach is typically beneficial to a newer salesperson or someone who lacks experience or is new to a task. When they know what to do, they will take action quicker, are more confident, and will achieve results faster. It also saves time and reduces

Account Executive Action Steps for Next GSM	Date
Attend 4 networking events > 3 contacts per	5/1
Make 20 calls per day > 4 prospects > set 1 meeting	5/1
Daily LinkedIn: 3 connection requests, 1 intro, 1 meeting	5/1
Host a client recognition event for 20 clients at the Getty Museum.	5/15
Sales Manager Action Steps for Next GSM	Date
Spend day in the field going on meetings	4/21
Attend client event, help meet & greet, engage key clients	5/15

Figure 5.7   Setting Action Steps

the probability of wasting time while they try to figure out what to do on their own. The downside of the "telling" strategy, if you use it with experienced salespeople, is that they may get defensive; they believe they don't need to be told what to do, they already know what to do, even if they are not doing it. They may feel that they do not need that level of direction. They might not take that much ownership because they did not come up with the action steps on their own. Therefore, holding them accountable to executing a plan they did not create becomes more challenging.

With the asking strategy, you will use questions that draw from a salesperson's experience and strengths to gather their ideas for the action steps. The benefits of this are very empowering. They are able to create their own action steps and, as a result, be more likely to do them. It's a lot less challenging to hold them accountable because they created the plan. It also allows them to use their own creativity, which enhances ownership. In contrast, if you use the "asking" strategy with a salesperson who lacks experience or is new to the role, it could be more difficult for them to create viable action steps to help them achieve their goals. There are times when a salesperson is new to a role or a task and does not know what they do not know. In this case, the telling strategy is much more effective when creating action steps.

Versatile sales managers are able to easily move between the two styles and adapt the appropriate approach to each salesperson on their team. It's always optimal if salespeople can readily self-identify opportunities and action steps (because it is psychologically uplifting and it reflects their understanding of the sales process and methodology); if not, you will need to be more actively engaged in setting action steps for them.

Here are a few transition statements you could use when implementing the "telling" strategy:

> *I have a couple of ideas that I think might help. Would you like me to share them with you?*
>
> *This is what I think you might try ...*
>
> *Some other successful salespeople on the team have done this ...*
>
> *Best practices are ...*

Here are a few questions you could use when implementing the "asking" strategy:

> *What do you need to change?*
>
> *What can you do differently?*
>
> *What have you done in the past that has worked?*
>
> *What do you want to start, stop, or keep doing?*

In many situations through the art of conversation, developing action steps with a salesperson is a dance. It's a combination of asking and telling. The key is to know when and how to "ask" and when and how to "tell." What you don't want to do is give the impression that "It's my way or the highway."

> *Adaptability is the ability to adjust to any situation at any given time.*
> —UCLA basketball coach John Wooden

Clear Action Steps for the Salesperson As you and your salesperson work together to construct the action steps, it is critical that the plan is goal-oriented. If they have the right plan and execute it well, they should achieve 100% of their goals. If the plan is not well conceived, a salesperson could have 100% execution of the plan but not hit their goals. Here is a formula you can use to help put quality action steps together: day, time block, activity goal, desired outcome.

Many sales managers who are trying to maintain their level of fitness could relate to an action step like the following for a Monday morning.

Day: Monday 5:00–6:30 a.m.

Time blocks and activities: gym 5:00–6:00 a.m. – run 6 miles on treadmill; 6:00–6:15 a.m. – foam roller and stretch; legendary abs 6:15-6:30 a.m.

Desired outcome: maintain fitness.

Here are some sales management examples:

- Attend four networking events per month with a goal of meeting five new people per event.
- Get on LinkedIn every day from 7:30 to 8:00 a.m., send five connection requests, ask one connection for a meeting and ask one connection for an introduction.
- Contact clients every day between 10:00 and 11:00 a.m. with a goal of making five contacts to set up one review meeting.
- Every day from 9:00 to 10:30 a.m. make 50 outbound calls with a goal of contacting five prospects and setting one meeting.

When it comes to collaborating with a salesperson on your team and you are asking questions to help them create action steps, you will need to coach them through the process of defining actions steps in very specific terms. If you do an effective job of this up-front, after several goal-setting meetings your sales team will be very good at creating their own action steps. At the beginning, when you ask them "What are you going to do to hit your goals?," you need to be prepared for them to say things like "I need to get more organized." "I am going to manage my time better." "I'm going to make more calls." "I'm going to work harder." "I'm going to work smarter." "I need to ask for more referrals." You get the idea.

The way you will coach them to develop specific action steps is by asking insightful questions. For example, you may use questions such as:

What's your plan?

What day do you want to do that?

What time in that day is the best for a time block to get that done?

What activity do you want to do in that time block?

What is your activity goal for that time block?

What results do you want to achieve?

You are going to rinse and repeat these questions until you and your salesperson have developed action steps that you both agree will enable the salesperson to reach their goals. The way you end setting action steps with your salesperson is to ask them this question: "Are these action steps doable; and, if you do all of these action steps we have outlined today, will you hit all of your goals?" This is a check point for both you and your salesperson, to determine if you created a solid action plan that is in alignment with goal achievement. If the answer to that question is "No," you need to revise the quality and/or quantity of the action steps.

Clear Action Steps for the Sales Manager During the goal-setting meeting you may discover that your salesperson has either a skill gap or a will/attitude issue that is limiting their ability to achieve their goals. If they have a skill gap, it may require that you set some time on your calendar to do some skill development training. You can also schedule time either in the field or deskside to watch them in action and deliver performance feedback. If your salesperson is falling short of their goals because they lack the will, one thing you can do is increase the frequency of the goal-setting meetings.

Now that you have documented the salesperson's action steps on the goal-setting meeting form, you will transition into determining if there is any type of support, coaching advice, or training they may want from you to help them achieve their goals. The question you may want to ask is, "What support do you need from me to help you to achieve your goals?"

You may hear general responses such as "Just drop by and ask me how I'm doing." "Check in with me over the course of the month." The challenge with any of these statements is that the salesperson has the right intent, their heart is in the right place, yet there is no real specificity on precisely how they would like you to support them in reaching their goals. There may be other times when a salesperson is very specific about the type of support they would like to see from you. For example, "Could you help me prepare a proposal for the upcoming meeting with ABC company?" "Could we do a dry run together for the recommendation meeting I will be conducting next Monday?" "Can you sit deskside with me and listen to me make some calls and give me feedback on how I'm doing?"

Depending on the salesperson's response, whether general or specific, you will want to ask questions to gain clarity around how you can support them, which will help in creating your action steps. Below are examples of things a salesperson might say, along with clarifying responses from the sales manager.

Salesperson: Just drop by and ask me how I'm doing.
Sales manager: Is there anything in particular you are working on that you would like my input or feedback on?

Salesperson: Check in with me over the course of the month.
Sales manager: If I were to check in with you over the course of the month, what would that look like?

Salesperson: I want you to listen to my pitch.
Sales manager: If I were to listen to your pitch, what would you like to see happen?

Salesperson: Could we do a dry run together for the recommendation meeting I will be conducting next Monday?
Sales manager: When do you want to do that? How much time do you think we'll need?

Here are some example action steps for the sales manager:

- Spend day in the field going on meetings – January 23.
- Attend client recognition event on January 17 and help with meet and greet and engage key clients in conversation.
- Meet for one hour on January 10 – dry run for recommendation meeting.

We know that most salespeople would like their sales manager to be more engaged in the activities they are doing. They feel that when the sales manager is engaged with them and gives them feedback on what they are doing, they are going to do better at their job.

Step 4: Summarize, Gain Commitment, and Set Next Meeting

After you and your salesperson complete the task of developing action steps that fit the S.M.A.R.T. formula, you will move to step 4: summary and commitment. This is a critical step, because it is easy for salespeople (and sales managers) to forget all these great ideas as soon as the next email/phone call/text message comes in.

Sales manager: [Salesperson's name], to make sure we're on the same page, let's summarize the action steps we came up with today. Walk me through your plan.

Salesperson recaps their action steps.

Sales manager: Thanks [salesperson's name]. Now, what I'm going to do to support you is ...

Sales manager recaps their action steps.

Sales manager: Are we in agreement? Now, let's get the date and time for our next goal-setting meeting on the calendar.

Date and time are agreed to and put on both the sales manager and salesperson's calendars.

Sales manager: Now, let's both sign and date the form.

Date and time for next goal-setting meeting are added to the form and both the sales manager and the salesperson sign the form.

The goal-setting meeting is coming to a conclusion and you want to make sure you are both clear on the action steps that are expected to be executed before the next goal-setting meeting; that is why it's important for each of you to summarize your action steps. When you put the date and time of the next goal-setting meeting on the form and both the sales manager and the salesperson sign it, something magical happens. It creates a greater sense of ownership, commitment, and urgency to take action immediately after the meeting. Here is what **not** to say:

> I've got a lot on my plate. I'm really busy. When I have a better idea of my schedule in a few weeks, I'll let you know when we can schedule our next meeting. I don't know when that might be, but I'll keep you posted.

Let's examine what this communicates to the salesperson. It demonstrates that the goal-setting meeting is not a priority and the salesperson's time is not as valuable as yours and the process begins to lose credibility. Over time, it could diminish your relationship with your sales team. The byproduct of that is that the salesperson has no general sense of urgency to get out and swing into action and begin working their plan. Oftentimes, when there is no date and time on the calendar, some salespeople will coast through the month until they find out when the next goal-setting meeting will be.

Without commitment, nothing happens.

—T. D. Jakes

Step 5: Give Encouragement

After you have signed and dated the form and agreed on the date and time for the next goal-setting meeting, you want to give encouragement to your salesperson. Let them know that you are behind them 100% and you are confident they can reach their goals.

Sales manager: This has been a great meeting. Don't you agree? I feel really good about the goals and action steps we've put down here and I am confident these steps will enable you to reach all your goals. You've got a great attitude and seem really motivated to make it happen. Go get 'em tiger!!! ROAR!

Every goal-setting meeting should generate some positive feelings, even if a salesperson is not meeting their targets for activities or

Goal-Setting Meeting

Name Mark Norman   **Date** 4/1

Biggest Victory Since Last GSM

Success starting every meeting with printed agenda. Prospects liked that I was prepared. Good feedback from sending Executive Summary within 24 hours of the meeting – actually landed a $300,000 opportunity!

Action Steps from Last GSM	Completion %
Attend 4 networking events > 3 contacts per	25%
Make 20 calls per day > 4 prospects > set 1 meeting	75%
Daily LinkedIn: 3 connection requests, 1 intro, 1 meeting	100%
Ask for referral at 4 recommendation meetings this month	100%

Key Performance Indicators	Goal	Actual	(+/-)	Next Goal
Contacts	80	60	-20	80
Connection meetings	20	15	-5	20
Discovery meetings	8	6	-2	8
Recommendation meetings	4	3	-1	4
New relationships opened	2	1	-1	2
Revenue	250,000	300,000	50,000	250,000

Observations

Great job last month using meeting agendas and executive summaries. You made 1 networking event and 4 meaningful contacts but fell short of 4 events due to a lot of time on the large opportunity. Great job with your calls but came up a short of your contact goal due to extra time preparing the proposal. You were very consistent with LinkedIn activity in the morning every day. Nice work asking for referrals at your recommendation meetings. You got 2 introductions in your target market.

Account Executive Action Steps for Next GSM	Date
Attend 4 networking events > 3 contacts per	5/1
Make 20 calls per day > 4 prospects > set 1 meeting	5/1
Daily LinkedIn: 3 connection requests, 1 intro, 1 meeting	5/1
Host a client recognition event for 20 clients at the Getty Museum.	5/15

Sales Manager Action Steps for Next GSM	Date
Spend day in the field going on meetings	4/21
Attend client event, help meet & greet, engage key clients	5/15

Next GSM Date: 5/1   **Time:** 8:00 AM

Mark Norman   *Steve Johnson*

Account Executive Signature   **Sales Manager Signature**

Figure 5.8   A Completed Goal-Setting Form

outcomes. This happens because the process is collaborative, the dialogue is interactive, they know what the expectations are, and they know their sales manager supports them.

Addressing Attitude Issues on Your Team: The Classic Types

Sales teams are bound to have a few people on the team who can be described as being somewhat difficult. Everybody has their own unique personality, attitude, and style; yet dealing with certain salespeople seems to require more patience, tact, resolve, energy, and emotional intelligence. In some situations, they are flat out exhausting to deal with. Because of this it can be very easy to ignore their behavior just to avoid conflict. Because you avoid it, it can grow and fester over time, impacting not only you personally, but other sales team members as well. Over time, it can have a negative impact on the culture of your sales team, which could impact your team's performance.

The good news is that there are some things you can do to address the attitude issues that will benefit you, the salesperson, and the entire sales team. There are a wide variety of attitude issues that an individual member of your sales team might have. We're going to present six example attitude issues you may encounter and some ideas you can use to address those issues, keeping in mind that there are a lot more. You may recognize the following six personas.

Sales Self-Conscious Sam

- Allows his thoughts, feelings, and beliefs about prospecting to turn into avoidance behavior that limits him from taking action.
- Is embarrassed that he is "trying to sell" something and is coming off as being salesy and is concerned that people will perceive him that way.
- Is very concerned about what others think about him based on his occupation and sales approach.
- Is overly concerned about interrupting and imposing on others with his prospecting efforts and is over-accommodating and apologetic.

- Is resistant to training and coaching due to his belief that there is never the right time, the right script, or the right response.
- Is defensive because his inner dialogue sounds something like this: "I'd never say words like that. They sound too salesy." "I would never call anybody on Friday afternoon because nobody's working!"

Sales Self-Conscious Sam is actually very common, especially in an outside sales force where salespeople are generating and cultivating their own leads and opportunities. Basically, what is limiting their success is the inner dialogue going on in their own mind. It's their own self-talk. Have a conversation with Sam to explain:

- The bulk of the prospecting activities he will do is an interruption – it's just the way it works.
- When he's prospecting, he needs to believe in what he sells and that he's doing the prospect a favor by contacting them.
- The importance of positive self-talk and how he can re-engineer it to help him improve.
- How scripts can be a great resource when they are practiced over and over again, with words he is comfortable using, until he has internalized them.
- The benefit of setting incremental goals and getting a win under his belt to help him overcome his fear and discomfort. For example, 30 minutes of calls each day for a week, the next week increase to 60 minutes of calls. Self-consciousness will diminish over time and self-confidence will begin to replace it.

Bad-Behavior Bob

- Often late to work.
- Often late to meetings.
- Doesn't do what he says he's going to do.
- Doesn't follow up consistently.
- Misses deadlines.
- Takes long lunches.

This behavior can rub off on other team members and negatively impact your sales team's culture and performance. It also gives others an excuse when you need to speak with them about their behavior – they will point to Bad-Behavior Bob and say, "Well, he does that all the time." This type of behavior generally gets worse, not better, over time. The longer you wait to address the behavior, the worse it will get.

> *What you permit you promote. What you allow, you encourage. What you condone, you own.*
>
> —Anonymous

Here are some ideas for dealing with Bad-Behavior Bob:

- Have a one-on-one meeting with Bob. Prior to the meeting, gather any documentation of the specific behaviors and conduct that Bob has demonstrated.
- Plan your talking points for the issues you want to discuss and the questions you want to ask. For example: "What are your thoughts on missing your deadlines and long lunches? How do you think that is affecting your performance? When you do these things, how do you think other people on the sales team perceive you? How do you think your actions affect the sales team and our sales culture?"
- Redirect the behavior by asking Bob, "What do you think you need to start or stop doing to ensure that these things don't happen anymore? What type of feedback would you like from me if you keep on doing what you're doing?"

Victim Vicky

- Blames prospects/clients for poor results because they take too long to make a decision.
- Is convinced co-workers are sabotaging her success.
- Indirectly blames you for her low sales due to your lack of support.
- Blames problems on other people rather than taking ownership and personal responsibility for her own success.

Having a team member who relishes talking about all the ways they have been mistreated by customers, co-workers, and management to anyone who will listen (especially if they do it in a setting where others can hear) undermines morale on the team. Here are some ideas for dealing with Victim Vicky:

- Don't encourage the negativity.
- When she begins to talk about how nothing's working, redirect the conversation in a more positive direction by encouraging her to talk about the things that are working by asking, "What's going well? What did you do to create that success? See, Vicky? Some things are going well. Keep doing the things you're doing that are generating success and try focusing less on the things that aren't working."
- When she starts to blame someone for something, ask her if there's something that she could have done differently to correct the matter.
- Ask Victim Vicky, "Walk me through exactly what your co-workers are saying or doing that is impacting your success. Give me a specific instance where this happened. What could you possibly have done differently in that situation and what can you do if it happens again?"
- Ask Victim Vicky, "What would you like from me in terms of support to help you feel better about this situation – what specifically would that support look like?"
- Many times, salespeople like Victim Vicky feel they are not getting the recognition, appreciation, and accolades that they deserve. Be aware of and look for opportunities to deliver genuine and sincere praise and appreciation to Victim Vicky and encourage her to be more positive in the future.

Overconfident Owen

- While some salespeople may need to work on their confidence, Overconfident Owen is on the other end of the spectrum. He can be too confident in his skills.
- He talks louder than anyone at meetings and may often undermine his co-workers.
- When you offer advice on how to close a particularly difficult sale, he brushes you off and may even remind you that he's been doing this for years.
- He may refuse to work with new team members and sees himself as special.
- He only associates with people that he considers to be on his level.

Having one team member who sets themselves apart because they believe they are better, more experienced, and more competent than the rest of the team negatively affects the cohesiveness of the team. Here are some ideas for dealing with Overconfident Owen:

- Have a one-on-one meeting with Owen. Plan your talking points for the specific things you want to discuss and the questions you want to ask. "You talked over your peers in our meeting. You seem uncoachable when I try to offer ideas on how to approach opportunities. You resist helping new team members to succeed. You don't think they're going to make it, so you don't want to waste any of your time. What is your perception of your behavior in these situations? What do you think the sales team's perception is of your behavior in these situations? Based on that, what do you think you could start or stop doing in these situations?"

- Discuss his openness to become a peer-to-peer coach. Because Owen is successful and has experience, you believe he has potential to add a tremendous amount of value to the team in this capacity. You may broach the topic by asking some questions such as, "Owen, you are experienced, and you are successful. How open are you to doing some peer-to-peer coaching with other members of the sales team? How open are you to sharing what's working and some of your best practices at sales meetings/huddles? How open are you to having new hires on the team sit deskside/shadow you in the field to observe you in action so they can see what success looks like?" If Owen is interested, you have created an opportunity to develop his skill set to be a peer-to-peer coach, which is a win. Conversely, if he is not interested, at least you have addressed his attitude and made him aware of it, which is also a win.

Underconfident Ursula

- Constantly asks for your help or other salespeople's help in closing sales, regardless of her prior successes.
- Frequently asks you to be at her initial meetings with prospects because she fears that she may be ineffective in conducting the meeting well enough to motivate the prospect to move forward to the next step in the sales process.

- Is trapped in the most confining cage there is, continually comparing herself to others, which has undermined her own value and self-worth.
- Is annoying some of the other salespeople on the team because she regularly asks for assistance, which impacts their productivity.

While Underconfident Ursula aims to please and do a good job, her lack of confidence can hurt the team, especially when everyone is trying to meet their sales goals. Here are some ideas for dealing with Underconfident Ursula:

- Praise Ursula on her strengths and give her affirmations to help her build her self-confidence. Confidence sells.
- Coach her to develop the ability to function in a more independent manner because there will be times when there will be no one to help her out.
- Provide skill development training to give her the opportunity to further develop her confidence and self-reliance.

Negative Nikki

- Has a habit of gossiping about executive leadership, the company, products and services, and co-workers.
- Is a naysayer – always talking about why things won't work as opposed to talking about how they could work.
- Takes a doomsday approach to a number of scenarios regarding the company.
- Is not supportive of other team members.

Being around negative people can be very detrimental to the fabric and culture of a sales team. Here are some ideas for dealing with Negative Nikki:

- Have a one-on-one meeting with Nikki and point out specific moments that you have documented when her attitude or statements had a negative impact on the sales team.
- Ask her why she has the sentiment she has toward the company, products, etc.
- Ask her to give you constructive ideas or input on how the things she's complaining about could be resolved or improved.

- Also, in this one-on-one meeting, you could ask Nikki if she is considering leaving the company – her negativity could be the byproduct of the fact that she already has one foot out of the door. There is a high degree of probability that Nikki will not be forthcoming with that information; but you at least put the topic on the table to gauge her reaction. If that were to be the case, it might be in your best interest to let her go.
- If the straw breaks the camel's back and she's just too toxic for your work environment, you will experience addition through subtraction by moving her on to another opportunity that may be more suitable to her skills and abilities.

You may notice a common thread among all these suggestions for addressing attitude issues with salespeople on your team. A best practice is to have a one-on-one conversation with the salesperson and, through asking questions, discuss the observable behaviors that you have seen that are the end result of the underlying attitude issue. Once you and the salesperson have agreed that there is an opportunity for improvement, you will then formulate action steps around what your salesperson should stop, start, or keep doing.

Keep in mind that a salesperson who is achieving their goals may still have an issue that is not based on skill or will, but attitude. The attitude issue they have at times is less about how it affects their performance, and more about how it affects you, the rest of the sales team, and your culture. It is also possible for a salesperson who has no skill gap or will issue to not be meeting their goals. It is solely their attitude that is holding them back. That's why you're there. Whether it's skill, will, or attitude, your role is to identify their opportunity for improvement and then help them to put a plan in place to close that gap.

Goal-Setting Meeting Best Practices

There are a variety of metrics that indicate employee engagement and employee job satisfaction, especially with their manager. Many of the most important elements of what employees want out of their job could be addressed if their manager had consistent goal-setting meetings with them. Many large studies have found that continual coaching has a powerful impact on performance. Goal setting has a stronger positive effect on performance when it is accompanied by feedback on progress. In every goal-setting meeting, there is recognition for successes, a conversation about progress on action steps, about expectations and performance, support offered from the manager, and finally, encouragement. If the only coaching activity you ever did was to conduct consistent goal-setting meetings with every salesperson on your team, you would be ahead of the game. Here are some tips that will help you to do just that.

- Following up between goal-setting meetings is extremely important. You can check in either formally or informally between goal-setting meetings. We will cover this in more detail in Chapter 7.

> *Specific is terrific!*
> —Steve Johnson

- Be as precise as you can in creating action steps. The more specific, the better.
- Every salesperson can benefit from coaching. Just because you have an "A" player does not mean that you should just leave them alone. In our experience, the performance of "A" players increases at a greater rate with coaching than "C" players.
- Set aside time on a consistent basis for your goal-setting meetings. Most successful sales managers have standing appointments with their team for goal-setting meetings.
- Document and keep your goal-setting meeting forms or data. Organize the goal-setting meetings by salesperson so an entire year of forms will be grouped together in one spot to track the progress of each salesperson. Being organized in this way will really help in your preparation time between goal-setting meetings.
- Conduct the goal-setting meeting in a professional setting, which is free of distractions such as telephones, computers, visitors, etc.
- As the sales manager, you control the goal-setting meeting form. You fill it in as the meeting progresses.
- Try to avoid having your salesperson fill in the form as a time-saving device for yourself. The act of them filling it in is basically them filling in their own performance review.

- If salespeople are not hitting the goals, spend more time focusing on developing action steps to achieve the goals as opposed to negotiating what the goals should be. Don't change the goal, change the plan. It's a goal-setting meeting, not a negotiation meeting.
- When the meeting is over, give your salesperson a copy of the goal-setting meeting form and encourage them to put it in a place that is visible as a constant reminder of what to do.
- Encourage your salesperson to take the goal-setting meeting form back to their desk and immediately time block their action steps in their calendar.
- In a goal-setting meeting you are also able to schedule other follow-up activities such as sitting deskside, spending a day in the field with them, or a pipeline review.
- Become highly effective at documenting the conversations on the form and saving the forms because you never know what's going to happen and you never know when you might need them. It never hurts to have a documented paper trail about conversations on sales performance.

Takeaway Questions

Below are questions you can use for further reflection.

Takeaway Discussion Questions for Your Organization

- If you are leading a sales organization, are all of your sales managers conducting consistent goal-setting meetings with every direct report under them in the organization?
- If yes, how consistent and effective are they?
- If no, why not?

Takeaway Questions for Personal Reflection

- If you are leading a sales team, what is your opportunity for improvement for conducting goal-setting meetings?

6

Skill Development Training

If you're not humble, it's hard to be coached. If you can't be coached, it's hard to get better.
—Jay Wright, Head Men's Basketball Coach, Villanova University

Skill Development Training

EVERY FOUR YEARS people around the world enjoy watching the Olympic Games, both winter and summer, knowing it took the participants years of training, practice, and sacrifice to develop world-class skills. In fields as diverse as athletics, the performing arts, and the military, we take it for granted that participants spend the majority of their time training and practicing so that, when the moment comes, they execute flawlessly under pressure.

In the broader world of sports, we are pretty confident that winning coaches hold practices, observe games, give feedback, and help their team enhance their performance. You would also expect that their players would be open – in fact, eager – for feedback on what they could do better in order to improve. Their best players not only practice with the team, they typically also have their own personal training regimen and personal trainer as well. For example, Tom Brady, who has won six NFL championships with the New England Patriots, has his own personal trainer, Alex Guerrero.

Some sales organizations make the mistake of assuming this doesn't apply to them, or that only new hires need training. Sales skills are like any other skills: those who practice their skills regularly and receive solid coaching and feedback are going to get better over time and produce superior results. Those who don't will probably continue to perform at the same level they always have; but, if they were able to address their skill gaps through practice, they could potentially improve their results.

Talent is Overrated

Where does greatness come from? How do individuals and organizations produce uncommon results? Is it nature, or is it nurture? Geoffrey Colvin's analysis of greatness, *Talent is Overrated* (Colvin 2010) reveals a pattern: individuals who achieve more do things differently than everyone else:

- They practice more.
- They build mental maps of their work.
- They consistently engage in deliberate practice that is just beyond their comfort zone.
- They seek continual feedback.

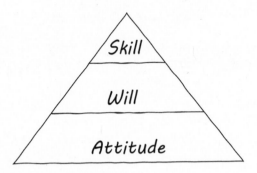

Figure 6.1 Skill–Will–Attitude

Everyone takes it for granted that the best orchestras and athletic teams spend most of their time practicing – that is what makes them the best. Oftentimes, we seem to forget this when we get to work! When does the practice start in order to develop your sales skills? Does the practice ever end as you strive to continue to polish your sales skills?

In our experience, there are three key ingredients for success in sales: skill, will, and attitude. You need to hire the salespeople who you believe have the talent to be successful. Then, you need to train and coach them, so they are able to develop their ability and turn it into a skill. This requires practice. Then, they need to have the will to apply those skills every single day to achieve their goals – all the while possessing the attitude that, when they are implementing those skills, they will get the results they are looking for.

Skill, will, and attitude work synergistically with each other. When salespeople become more skilled through practice, it can potentially impact their motivation to succeed and will build two traits that are essential to success in sales: enthusiasm and confidence. In the absence of well-developed sales skills, salespeople achieve poor performance, can get demotivated, and that can negatively affect their attitude. From our experience, this produces poor results. Generally speaking, if a salesperson has a positive attitude, it can increase their will to practice their skills and enhance their motivation to apply those skills to achieving their goals.

The separation of talent and skill is one of the biggest misconceptions for salespeople who are trying to succeed in a career that could potentially provide them a true path to compensation that is based

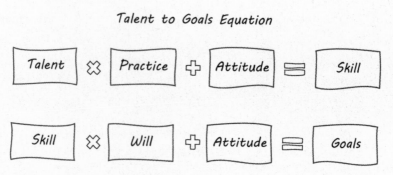

Figure 6.2   Talent-to-Goals Equation

on their value. Talent they possess naturally. Their sales skill will only be developed by hours of intentional, purposeful, and relentless practice. Having talent is not enough to ensure a salesperson will hit their goals. Without practice, talent is nothing more that unmet potential. Without the will to develop the skills to achieve their goals, skill is nothing more than what a salesperson could have done but didn't. But with the right attitude, talent developed through practice becomes skill and, at the very same time, will make skill productive.

Skill Development Training Challenges

Here are some reasons that sales managers don't train/reinforce skills, or don't do it effectively or consistently:

- Sales manager lacks sales skills and ability to train and reinforce sales skills.
- Sales manager lacks confidence in their ability to demonstrate and coach skills.
- It takes time.
- It is repetitive and can be boring.
- It requires getting salespeople out of their comfort zones.
- Sales manager hasn't been trained on how to do it.
- Sales manager has not built skill development training into their routine.
- Sales manager fears the sales team will resist training.

As you read through these eight statements as to why sales managers resist doing skill development training with their sales teams, think about which one of these reasons resonates with you.

Benefits of Skill Development Training

When salespeople improve their skills, in an ideal scenario it could positively improve their performance. When performance improves, morale improves, which could contribute to a higher retention rate. When training happens in a team setting, it builds team spirit and gives the sales team the opportunity to practice with and learn from each other. Training builds confidence and enthusiasm, which are very important in sales.

> *The more you learn, the more you earn.*
> —Steve Johnson

You bought and are reading this book, you made it this far. If you are not doing regular skill development training with your sales team, why not start now? Some salespeople may resist or get defensive. People don't like change because it gets them out of their comfort zone. Communicate to your sales team what you are doing, why you're doing it, and how they will benefit. Let them know that you want to improve as a sales manager because you feel that, if you do, you can help them improve their sales skills. As they get better, they will be moving forward with their career in sales, while also impacting customers and helping the company achieve its goals. *Salespeople improve when sales management improves: When you get better, they get better.*

Opportunities for Skill Development Training

Whenever you are training for skill development, only focus on **one** skill at a time to maximize effectiveness. Many sales managers try to accomplish way too much as opposed to isolating one thing to work on. In other words, less is more.

Within a goal-setting meeting, you may identify a skill gap in one of your salespeople that is limiting their ability to achieve their goals and decide to address the gap with skill development training within the framework of the goal-setting meeting. If you find yourself consistently doing skill development training in goal-setting meetings, you will need to build the time for that in your meeting agenda.

For example, as you are discussing the key performance indicators (KPIs) in the meeting, you may uncover that their conversion ratio of contacts to meetings is low. You have identified that the skill gap is in handling the objection: "I'm happy with my current supplier." You could transition into skill development training by saying something like the following.

Sales manager: [Salesperson's name], what we're going to work on is how to handle the objection of "I'm happy with my current supplier." Why this is important to you is, as we look at your KPIs we notice that your conversion rate from contacts to meetings is low and, if you could increase your conversion rate by strengthening your ability to overcome that objection, it would improve your probability of success. Here is how we're going to do it: I am going to explain how to handle that objection. Then, I will demonstrate what a response to that objection might sound like. Then we will practice – I will go and then you will go. We will go back and forth until you have your response to the point where you feel confident in your ability to use it when presented with that objection. I'll observe you and give you feedback as you practice to help you get better, faster. When we're done, you will have the opportunity to give me a demonstration of what we worked on to make sure that you got it. How does that sound?

You may also identify opportunities to conduct skill development training when you are doing check-ins with your salespeople throughout the week or month, following up on goals and action steps from the goal-setting meeting. When you ask them, "How are things going," they may indicate a challenge they are facing which would provide an opportunity to dive into a skill development interaction.

Alternatively, you may decide to train/reinforce sales skills with your team within a sales meeting or a sales huddle. For example:

Sales manager: Team, what we're going to work on today is how to communicate the features and benefits of our new product line. Why this is important to you is because it is a brand-new line, our customers want to hear about it, and, the more confident and capable we are, the better we can get this new product line off the ground. Here is how we're going to do it: I will explain how to communicate the features and benefits of the new product line. Then, I will demonstrate what it might sound like. Then we will practice – I will go and then you will go. We will go back and forth until you feel confident in your ability to use the features, bridges, and benefits of the new product line in conversations with our customers. I'll observe you and give you feedback as you practice to help you get better, faster. When we're done, you will have the opportunity to give me a demonstration of what we worked on to make sure that you got it. How does that sound?

In most professional sporting events, athletes warm up before they play the game. When co-selling or conducting live observation for the purpose of delivering performance feedback, you can also include skill development training as part of your pre-call/meeting preparation. This is a particularly effective time to practice skills because it allows you and the salesperson you are coaching to do a dry run/dress rehearsal and literally get warmed up for the call/meeting you are about to conduct. For example:

Sales manager: [Salesperson's name], what we're going to practice before we go into the meeting is how to set the agenda. Why this is important to you is because, when you start the meeting confidently with the agenda, the prospect will perceive that you are organized, professional, and value their time. As a result, they may be more engaged in the meeting. Here is how we're going to do it: I am going to explain how to set the agenda for the meeting. Then, I will demonstrate what it might sound like. Then we will practice – I will go and then you will go. We will go back and forth until you feel confident in your ability to set the agenda for today's meeting. I'll observe you and give you feedback as you practice to help you get better, faster. When we're done, you will have the opportunity to give me a demonstration of what we worked on to make sure that you got it. So, when we go into today's meeting, you are going to get this meeting started on the right foot. How does that sound?

You can also do skill development training when you are delivering performance feedback after a sales interaction when you identified a skill gap. This might be the optimal time to dive into skill development training because it was just recently observed. For example:

Sales manager: [Salesperson's name], looks like we agree you could have been more effective in the meeting with presenting your value proposition. While we're here right now and it's fresh in our mind, there is no time like the present to take advantage of the opportunity to practice your value proposition. It just happened and it could have gone better. What we're going to work on is your value proposition. Why this is important to you is because it will help you to develop the ability to more confidently state our capabilities and how our prospects can potentially benefit from forming a relationship with us. Here is how we're going to do it. First, I am going to explain how to communicate the value proposition. Then, I will demonstrate what it might sound like. Then, we will practice – I will go and then you will go. We will go back and forth until you feel confident in your ability to communicate your value proposition anytime, anywhere, with anybody. I'll observe you and give you feedback as you practice to help you get better, faster. When we're done, you will have the opportunity to give me a demonstration of what we worked on to make sure that you got it. How does that sound?

Good sales managers are very proactive and consistently look for opportunities to have these types of interactions with members of their sales team every day.

Skill Development Training Steps

As a parent, imagine training one of your children how to crack an egg so they are able to make their own breakfast. You would probably begin with some type of an explanation and then show them how to do it. Let's assume they are making an omelet which requires multiple eggs. After you demonstrate how to crack the first egg, you will observe them cracking the next egg to make sure they get it right. (After all, who wants to eat an omelet full of eggshells?) While they are cracking their egg, you will be observing them and giving them feedback, if necessary, to ensure they are able to crack eggs properly so that they can make their own omelets. (The real question is, after they learn to crack an egg and make their own omelet, are they going to clean up after and do the dishes?) It could sound something like this:

Parent: What we're going to work on today is how to crack an egg for an omelet. Why that's important to you is because you indicated you would like to be more independent and be able to make your own breakfast. How we're going to do this is simple. First, I am going to explain how to crack an egg. Then, I will demonstrate it for you, which is important if you want an omelet. Because we're going to make a four-egg omelet, you will practice by cracking the next egg. Then I'll crack the third egg and you'll practice by cracking the fourth egg. We will go back and forth until you feel confident in your ability to crack an egg to make an omelet. I'll observe you and give you feedback as you practice to help you get better at cracking eggs for an omelet. When we're done, you will have the opportunity to give me a demonstration of what we worked on to make sure that you got it. How does that sound?

This skill development training process is quite common when it comes to coaching, building, and reinforcing skills. It would be similar in a golf lesson, a piano lesson, or a skiing lesson. Even though the process is common, it is not commonly applied. When you put it to work in your sales coaching, you will see your sales team making rapid strides.

Step 1: Explain

This step of skill development training is important, because if you do it right, you will generate enthusiasm from the salespeople you are

Skill Development Training Steps

Figure 6.3   Skill Development

working with. Prior to the start of a skill development session, many salespeople may be asking themselves these three questions:

1. **What** are we going to work on?
2. **Why** is it important for me to do this?
3. **How** are we going to do this?

The reason they are asking themselves these questions is that they want to make sure that whatever the skill development session is covering will be worth their time. A lot of their time has been wasted in the past because their sales manager has been ineffective at training, coaching, and reinforcing skills. As a result, they have become resistant to giving up more of their time. Explaining what, why, and how helps connect the dots between what will be done in the skill development training and the three questions that pre-exist in the sales team's mind prior to engaging in the exercise. An opportunity for improvement for many sales managers is in how they position the explanation of what they will be working on with either their entire sales team in a meeting, or in a one-on-one skill development session with one of their salespeople.

The three things you typically explain are:

1. **What** skill you will be working on.
2. **Why** developing that skill is important to them.
3. **How** you will be conducting the skill development training.

Following these three steps in your explanation will enable you to set the agenda for the skill development training you will be going through with the salesperson. Here is an example focused on the skill of delivering customized features and benefits.

Sales manager: What we are going to work on today is how to use features and benefits in a way that is customized to a prospect's needs that we have uncovered based on our discovery questions. **Why** this is important to you is because, when you link specific features and benefits back to a customer's wants, needs, and motives, your presentation will be more targeted, motivating, and specific to their situation. They will be better able to see themselves using, enjoying, and benefiting from our product. **How** we're going to do this is, first, I will explain to you how to communicate customized features and benefits. Then, I will demonstrate how to use them in the fabric of a presentation so you can hear what they sound like. Then we will practice – I will go and then you will go. We will go back and forth until you feel confident in your ability to communicate customized features and benefits, anywhere, with anybody. I'll observe you and give you feedback as you practice in order to help you get better, faster. When we're done, you will have the opportunity to give me a demonstration of what we worked on to make sure that you got it. How does that sound?

Repetition is the mother of learning.

—Ancient Latin inscription

Here is another example, this time asking for a referral.

Sales manager: What we are going to work on today is how to ask for a referral after you have landed an opportunity with a new customer. **Why** this is important to you is because there is no better time to ask for a referral than right after you have completed the paperwork with the new customer. The reason is that the customer feels good about the decision they just made and may be willing to refer others to you. **How** we will do this is, first, I will explain to you how to ask for a referral. Then, I will demonstrate how to do it so you can hear what it sounds like. Then we will practice – I will go and then you will go. We will go back and forth until you feel confident in your ability to ask for referrals right after you land a new opportunity. I'll observe you and give you feedback as you practice to help you get better, faster. When we're done, you will have the opportunity to give me a demonstration of what we worked on to make sure that you got it. How does that sound?

In the example above, after you have communicated the what, the why, and the how, you could easily spend 10 straight minutes going back and forth practicing, refining, practicing, refining, how to ask for a referral. The reason this does not happen is that many sales managers are able but unwilling to invest that amount of time going back and forth with practice. The primary reason behind that is that repetitive practice is boring; and, the fact of the matter is, success is boring. Successful people have cultivated good habits which have been developed over time. They do the same things repeatedly, without even thinking about it. One way they have formed those habits is through their dedication to practice. Lack of success is also boring. Unsuccessful people have bad habits and continue to do the same things that don't work repeatedly, without thinking about it. One way to cultivate good habits is through repetitive practice. When salespeople are under pressure, they fall back on what is familiar. Hopefully, what is familiar is what they have practiced relentlessly with their sales manager.

Don't practice till you get it right. Practice till you can't get it wrong.
—Anonymous

Step 2: Demonstrate

Nothing beats a good demonstration when you are training, coaching, and reinforcing skills with your sales team. During your demonstration, you want your salespeople to be observing and absorbing exactly what success looks like. Typically, a salesperson is able to perform the skill at the level of effectiveness at which they have observed it. In other words, the better you demonstrate the skill, the more motivated your salesperson will be to want to practice the skill so they can become as good in that skill as you are. They believe that implementing the skill at a high level will help them improve performance. A flawless demonstration is one of the most important, fundamental ways you can help your sales team further develop their skills.

With an excellent demonstration, you gain credibility and buy-in from your team. In contrast, an ineffective demonstration will not only set a bad example, it will also diminish the motivation to practice the skill and apply it on the job. Through our experiences we have found that most sales organizations that have a sales process and a sales methodology built that process and methodology around the best practices of their top performers. Those best practices are typically words, talking points, transition phrases, and responses to objections that high achievers use because they work in their environment. It is tribal knowledge that has been proven to lead to superior results. This information typically gets synthesized into some type of a script, meeting template, job aid, or call flow. The single best source of information is through top performers. Many times, these resources are used in onboarding training and in coaching and reinforcing skills with tenured salespeople. It is not uncommon for a sales manager to use these existing talking points/scripts when giving demonstrations in skill development training. It doesn't mean that you must always use scripts/talking points in your demonstrations with your sales team, but they are a great starting point.

Resistance to Scripting Even though these organizations know their methodology is built on best practices supported with scripts and talking points, it is surprising that so many salespeople are still resistant to practicing scripts that are used by top performers in their own company.

Let's assume you are conducting skill development training either in a one-on-one setting or with the entire sales team and you want to utilize a script in your demonstration. Some of your salespeople may react emotionally, either out loud or to themselves, with:

Don't cramp my style!

I don't want to sound scripted.

I don't want to sound robotic.

I don't want to sound salesy.

I don't talk like that.

I don't want to sound like I work in a call center.

What they may fail to appreciate is, they are already scripted! They say the same things over and over again, just like they wear the same clothes 80% of the time and eat the same food 80% of the time. Everyone already has habits; the question is, how effective are the scripts they are using now?

The Benefits of Scripting   Singers sing lyrics. Sports teams run plays. Dancers do routines. Actors use scripts. They practice them so many times it becomes who they are. In sales, unlike on Broadway, you don't expect your salespeople to deliver the exact same lines in every performance, but you do expect them to practice using the scripts until they are so internalized that they will always deliver a fresh and compelling performance with confidence. If you don't like the idea of scripts, think of them as pre-memorized language. Think of them as a bridge to competence.

Scripts are an indispensable resource when doing demonstrations in skill development training because they:

- Are typically based on best practices of top performers.
- Give you a good starting point to work from.
- Give you something to practice.
- Can serve as a blueprint to refine and make your own.
- Build confidence in your sales team.
- Help you sound more natural when well-practiced.

Step 3: Practice

Some salespeople love to practice their skills. Others don't, which is hard to believe. After all, how are you ever going to get better or generate different results without practice? You play like you practice. When the game is on the line and the largest sales opportunity you have ever generated in your career is within your grasp, the notion that you will go in there and perform at a high level (that you have never simulated or performed before through rigorous practice) is absolutely ridiculous. It is highly unlikely that you will do something when you are in the spotlight that you have never done before. Many of your salespeople may not realize this, and this is why you must be persistent during the "Practice" step of the skill development process.

> *The four laws of learning are explanation, demonstration, imitation, and repetition. The goal is to create a correct habit that can be produced instinctively under great pressure. To make sure this goal was achieved, I created eight laws of learning namely: explanation, demonstration, imitation, repetition, repetition, repetition, repetition and repetition.*
> —UCLA basketball coach John Wooden

Imagine yourself as a coach of a sports team. One of your roles in practice is to run your team through drills. Well-conducted drills are uncomfortable. Why? Because they require focus, effort, and the right attitude for both you and your team. The purpose of the drill is to help your team build their skills and abilities to help them be competitive and win games. Practice helps winning. There is a correlation between practice and success.

Most sales managers are ineffective at skill development training because they are uncomfortable making their salespeople uncomfortable. The only one way to become great at conducting skill development training is to develop the mindset that you are doing it *for* them, you are not doing it *to* them. Because you are doing it for them, try to not react emotionally to their facial expressions while they are outside of their comfort zone, even though you may be tempted to take your foot off the gas pedal. Don't be deterred by their body language, their emotional reaction to repetitive practice, or their discomfort.

We have actually said something like the following to thousands and thousands of people whom we have trained and coached:

> We are not doing this to you, we're doing it for you. We are operating in your best interests. We understand that, if left to your own devices, you are not going to put in the deliberate, intentional, repetitive practice needed to master this skill. This is what we know to be true: When you are under pressure, you fall back on what is familiar. And you want the familiar to be something you have practiced the most, because we already know it works. It is my job to help you practice something that works so that no matter what happens, when you're under pressure, what comes out of you will be what you have practiced over and over until you have made it your own.

There is no growth in the comfort zone and no comfort in the growth zone.
—Steve Johnson

When conducting skill development training, take it one step at a time. Salespeople work very well with bite-size pieces of information. Ask yourself, "What is the single smallest element that I want to focus on first in this training session?" Then ask yourself, "What is the second skill, related to the first skill, that we can work on next?" Take a manageable piece and practice it in a deliberate manner so that you get dramatic improvement on one small skill at a time. In the practice step, remember:

- Be prepared to give several demonstrations if they need more help. Talk less, demonstrate more.
- You will be going back and forth with the salesperson you are practicing with, which means you will repeatedly be giving the same demonstration over and over again. You will tell the salesperson you are practicing with, "I'm going to go then you are going to go, then I'm going to go then you are going to go, etc." ad nauseum.
- The first practice repetitions your salesperson does are very important. Much like the grooves in a record, the way they repeatedly practice is the way they will play in the game.

- Go very slowly. Be exact and precise with the practice because the ultimate goal is to achieve consistency.
- While you are practicing back and forth, praise every improvement you see, look for the positive.
- Give constructive feedback in baby steps.
- If, while practicing, you observe an opportunity for improvement, attempt to fix that skill gap immediately.
- Be persistent – remember deliberate, purposeful, intentional practice will build the right type of skill.
- Be prepared to be bored out of your mind as you make the single best investment of your time in the skill development of your sales team. This investment over the long haul may be the best way to save you and your salespeople time. You will be anchoring the right skills up-front, instead of spending time later down the road trying to correct poor skills that have developed into bad habits that generate poor performance.
- The ultimate objective is for them to be able to demonstrate the skill so you know they are competent in the skill. Therefore, if they do not use this skill to generate positive sales results, it's not a skill issue, it's an attitude or will issue.

> *If disproportionate results come from one activity, then you must give that activity disproportionate time.*
>
> —Gary Keller

Step 4: Observe

As you and your salesperson practice together, you want to make sure you are observing every little detail of the practice: not just the words but the tone of voice, body language, facial expressions, and enthusiasm behind it. Early on, your primary focus will be on the elements of the practice that are done well, in addition to the opportunities for improvement. As you are doing repetitive practice and observing, you begin to look for higher levels of precision, confidence, and competency, so they will ultimately be able to perform the skill every time without thinking about it.

Once you feel your salesperson has developed this level of consistency while you are observing them through repetitive practice, observe them giving an uninterrupted demonstration of the skill. If the demonstration is delivered with the precision and competency you are looking for, proceed to feedback. If not, go back to either explain, demonstrate, or practice depending on how much additional work is needed to bring them to an acceptable level of competence.

You can observe a lot by just watching.

—Yogi Berra

Step 5: Feedback

When you are engaged in repetitive practice with your salesperson and you are observing them in action, there are three types of feedback you will probably be giving them – positive, reflective, and directive. Going back to the "I go, you go" notion of practice, you will be delivering these three types of feedback in small pieces in between each of the back-and-forth practice. Let us give you an example of what this might look like. Let's assume that you were doing a skill development training session with one of your salespeople on how to handle objections to setting a face-to-face meeting and the response you were going to use for your demonstration was a very popular technique for responding to objections: "feel, felt, found."

First, the sales manager demonstrates "feel, felt, found" very slowly.

Sales manager: Patrick, I understand how you **feel**. In fact, many of my clients, like you, **felt** the same way when I first contacted them. They went ahead and had a brief meeting with me and what they **found** was that I was able to add value to their situation. What's better for you, morning or afternoon?

Then, the sales manager continues.

Sales manager: Did you hear how slowly I demonstrated "feel, felt, found?" The reason is, in all the time I have trained and coached salespeople I've noticed that, when they are learning, practicing, or reinforcing a skill, their natural tendency is to try to do it quickly. I understand that. We are going to start out practicing very slowly because it will help catch our errors quickly and fix them. Then, as we get better, the pace of our practice will become a little faster.

It's not how fast you can do it; it's how slowly you can do it correctly.
—Daniel Coyle

Sales manager: Now it's your turn. Go slowly.

The salesperson practices "feel, felt, found" slowly.

Sales manager: Great job. Way to get your first rep under your belt and stick to the format slowly.

The sales manager then demonstrates "feel, felt, found" again, slowly, and then asks the salesperson to go again. The salesperson practices the technique again, goes a little faster than they should, and it sounds a little choppy.

Sales manager: Nice work. Next time, try to do it a little slower again so you really get it down.

The sales manager demonstrates "feel, felt, found" again, emphasizing the slower pace to methodically demonstrate how to use the correct words and asks the salesperson to go again. The salesperson practices the technique again, a little slower, and it sounds better.

Sales manager: Nice upgrade going at a slower pace. You're really getting the words down better. Let's do it one more time, slowly, and try to add a little more voice tone and inflection, emphasizing the words "feel, felt, found." I'll go first and then you can go.

The sales manager then demonstrates the technique again, slowly, emphasizing the words "feel, felt, found" with voice tone and inflection. The manager asks the salesperson to go again and the salesperson practices the technique a little slower, focusing on improving their voice tone and inflection on the key words of "feel, felt, found."

Sales manager: Great job. Let's do it just like that, three times in a row. First, I'm going to go, then you're going to go, speaking slowly with emphasis on the three key words of "feel, felt, found."

They repeat the practice three times each, back and forth.

Sales manager: You know what? It's really beginning to sound just like you. You have personalized it, you've internalized it, and it does not sound like a script now. How do you feel about the progress you've made so far? Are you ready to give me some uninterrupted demonstrations of the technique to make sure you've got it down?

The salesperson demonstrates the technique again and reveals some room for improvement in their voice tone.

Sales manager: Think about your tone of voice that time. Is there anything you can think of that could improve it?

Salesperson: Well, because it's an objection I'm trying to handle, I could put more confidence in my voice tone to make it more compelling.

Sales manager: Agreed. That is a good self-assessment. Let's do it again with a little more confidence.

The salesperson does it again with improved confidence.

Sales manager: Well done, assimilating the feedback and communicating with more confidence. How about your pace? Would you say it was slow or fast?

Salesperson: I could have probably gone a little slower.

Sales manager: I think you're right. Try it again, a little slower this time.

The salesperson does it again, a little slower. The execution of the "feel, felt, found" response was flawless.

Sales manager: I think you got it! Why don't you do it one more time.

The salesperson does it one more time.

Step 6: Salesperson Demonstration

At the end of the skill development training session, it is important to have your salesperson demonstrate the skill you have been practicing. This test for competency will show they have developed the ability and proficiency necessary to apply the skill in a real-life sales situation. In short, the way to ensure they pass this test for competency is to have the attitude that the practice should be harder than the game. If you have had a world-class practice session, when it comes time for the salesperson to give a demonstration of the skill, it will be a slam-dunk. Let's revisit that dialogue one more time to illuminate the salesperson's demonstration as a test for competency.

Sales manager: Now, I'd like you to do a demonstration of using the technique to me as if I were a prospect who has just said they're not interested in meeting with you.

Salesperson (with poise and self-confidence): Mr. Johnson, I understand how you **feel**. In fact, many of my clients, like you, **felt** the same way when I first contacted them. They went ahead and had a brief meeting with me and what they **found** was that I was able to add value to their situation. What's better for you, morning or afternoon?

Sales manager: Thanks for that great demonstration. I want to compliment you on how open-minded and receptive you were to the repetitive practice that we've put in here today on how to handle an objection using "feel, felt, found." You really crushed it!

Types of Feedback in Skill Development Training

In the skill development training example above, you probably noticed the three types of feedback. Positive feedback is a way to compliment, appreciate, or reinforce a strength, skill, or attitude that encourages the salesperson you are working with to keep doing what they are

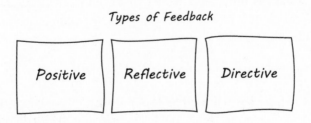

Figure 6.4   Types of Feedback

doing. It is very important in skill development training because it helps the salesperson build their skill, which affects their will and attitude and focuses on their strengths. Reflective feedback is a way to ask the salesperson you are practicing with questions that will elicit responses on things they might start, stop, or keep doing. Directive feedback is using more of the telling strategy where you would be recommending or suggesting what they might start, stop, or keep doing.

Here are some examples of **positive** feedback from the skill development training conversation:

- Great job. Way to get your first rep under your belt and stick to the format slowly.
- Nice upgrade going at a slower pace. You're really getting the words down better.
- You know what? It's really beginning to sound just like you. You have personalized it, you've internalized it, and it does not sound like a script now.
- Agreed. That is a good self-assessment.
- Thanks for that great demonstration. I want to compliment you on how open-minded and receptive you were to the repetitive practice that we've put in here today on how to handle an objection using "feel, felt, found." You really crushed it!

Here are some examples of **reflective** feedback:

- How do you feel about the progress you've made so far? Are you ready to give me some uninterrupted demonstrations on communicating the technique to make sure you've got it down?
- What do you think you can do to improve the confidence in your voice tone?
- Well done, assimilating the feedback and communicating with more confidence. How about your pace? Would you say it was slow or fast?

Here are some examples of **directive** feedback:

- Next time, try to do it a little slower again so you really get it down.
- Let's do it one more time, slowly, and try to add a little more voice tone and inflection, emphasizing the words "feel, felt, found."

- Let's do it again with a little more confidence.
- Try it again, a little slower this time.

We all need people who will give us feedback. That's how we improve.

—Bill Gates

Skill Development Training Tips

Here are some tips for delivering skill development training:

- Embrace repetition, which might require you (and your team) to change your attitude. Instead of looking at repetition as a lot of work, look at it as your most impactful means to an end.
- When you are practicing in a deliberate manner, the most important thing is quality repetitions of what you are practicing. Ten minutes of quality repetitions is better than 20 minutes of poor-quality repetitions.
- Just because a salesperson on your team has gotten a fast start, does not mean they have mastered the fundamental skills that will enable them to be successful over time. Oftentimes, early success is a very weak indicator of long-term success.
- When practicing skills with your sales team, slow it down – potentially slower than you can even imagine. When you practice slowly, you can see the skill gaps with a higher degree of clarity and are more readily able to address them through directive feedback so that they don't turn into bad habits that are more difficult to unlearn over time.

Takeaway Questions

Below are questions you can use for further reflection.

Takeaway Discussion Questions for Your Organization

- If you are leading a sales organization, your sales managers are most likely already conducting skill development training.

(*continued*)

(*continued*)

- If you were to give them feedback on how they were doing, what type of feedback would you give them?
- If your managers are not consistently delivering skill development training, what can you do to make it happen?

Takeaway Questions for Personal Reflection

- If you are leading a sales team, what is your opportunity for improvement in conducting skill development training with your sales team?

7

Check-Ins

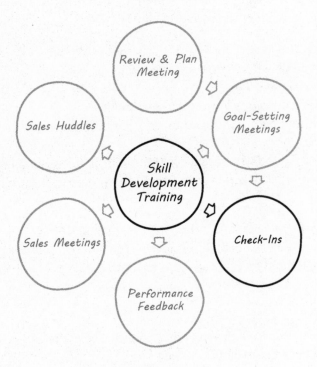

Check-Ins

LET'S ASSUME THAT you started the year with a review and plan, and you are conducting consistent goal-setting meetings with everyone on your sales team. When the opportunity presents itself, you are conducting skill development training in sales meetings or sitting deskside. One way to follow up on all these coaching activities is to do brief check-ins on a daily, weekly, or monthly basis to ensure that each member of your sales team is on the right track. These brief interactions allow you to engage with your sales team and create opportunities to give recognition on success, uncover obstacles, and create a greater connection with members of your team.

> *The key to greatness is to look for people's potential and spend time developing it.*
>
> —Peter Drucker

How Check-Ins Impact Your Sales Team in a Positive Way

What are many salespeople looking for in their work environment? According to Gallup (Clifton and Harter 2019, 17–19) they want:

- A sense of purpose in what they do, not just a job.
- Personal development, not job satisfaction.
- Coaches, not bosses.
- Ongoing conversations, not annual reviews.
- A sales manager who focuses on their strengths, not their weaknesses.
- Clarity around what is expected of them at work, not ambiguity.
- A sales manager who supports their development, not just demands results.

Through implementing the best-practice coaching tactics in this book, you will be able to address many of the priorities your sales team is looking for and meet those expectations.

Purpose

An annual review and plan meeting helps you to understand each team member's personal and business goals.

Development

Skill development training can and should happen in many of the situations we have covered in prior chapters. Developing your sales team on a career path from new hire to top performer to peer-to-peer coach helps deepens your bench of future leaders and gives them a path to mastery (Pink 2009).

Coaching

Adapting your approach to meet the individual needs of your salespeople, through using the asking/reflective, telling/directive styles in coaching, builds collaboration and enables them to identify their own opportunities, co-develop action steps, and take ownership of the plan and results. Implementing these coaching activities also shows your salespeople you are invested in their development. You are engaged in their growth and career path.

Conversations

Regular goal-setting meetings and check-ins provide structure for ongoing conversations that keep the team on track with the activities in place designed to help them achieve their goals.

Strengths

Finally, you should focus on your sales team's strengths by:

- Using tools such as CliftonStrengths, DISC, Myers Briggs, and Caliper to understand each individual's motivators and demotivators.
- Flexing your coaching and leadership style to meet the needs of each member of your sales team.
- Engaging in conversations with the theme of "What's going well? What's working?" and giving recognition based on the behaviors that are generating positive outcomes.
- Ending conversations with appreciation and encouragement.

People development should be a daily event, integrated into every aspect of your regular goings-on.

—Jack Welch

How to Check In

Consistent check-ins are a great way to keep conversations ongoing. One way to be successful at this is to proactively seek out formal and informal opportunities to check in with members of your sales team. Being proactive with check-ins enables you to:

- Catch salespeople doing something right and highlight their strengths.
- Share and invite good news.
- Invite ideas and opinions on relevant topics. For example, you are planning a regional sales meeting and would like input from your team on what type of speaker they think would be relevant and timely for the event.
- Have meaningful conversations with your sales team about what is going on outside of work – family, hobbies, vacation, etc.
- Provide a forum to reinforce messaging from sales meetings, review and plan meetings, goal-setting meetings, etc.
- Give individual attention to each salesperson.
- Uncover any obstacles or challenges they are facing.
- Take advantage of a just-in-time coaching opportunity.

Check-ins can happen through multiple modalities of communication such as: text, chat, video, voice, email, or conversations around the water cooler. How often should you check in? That depends on the tenure of the salesperson, their performance, the projects they're working on, the support they need, or the support they have requested from you.

In a contact center you may have the opportunity to conduct multiple check-ins per day just by walking around. If you are managing a remote team, you might be making calls or sending texts/emails; but let's say at a minimum once a week you are checking in.

Check-In Flow

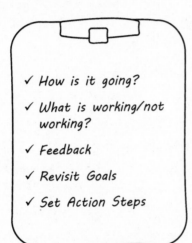

✓ How is it going?

✓ What is working/not working?

✓ Feedback

✓ Revisit Goals

✓ Set Action Steps

Figure 7.1   Check-In Agenda

In working with our clients, we have discovered that there is a wide variety of ways a sales manager can check in with members of their sales team on a daily, weekly, or monthly basis. It is very common for them to check in on action steps that were created in a goal-setting meeting.

> *When all is said and done, more is said than done.*
> —Lou Holtz

They typically do this with the following model. They first ask, "How's it going?" with respect to a specific goal or action step, then they dig deeper by asking questions about what's working/not working:

How's it going with your goal of _____?

What's working well for you?

What's not working for you?

Examples of Informal Check-Ins

There are endless ways for you to check in and stay connected with your sales team. Some check-ins are on a personal level, what's happening outside of work. Some are on key performance indicators and some are on goals. Others are simply around what's happening right now. Here are some example conversation starters you can use to engage your sales team in an informal check-in:

> *How was the sales meeting today?*
>
> *How many contacts did you make today?*
>
> *How is your pipeline going for the month?*
>
> *How was the new product training?*
>
> *How was the peer-to-peer coaching you got from Mike today as he sat deskside with you?*
>
> *How was your daughter's soccer game yesterday?*
>
> *Welcome back. How was your trip to Australia?*
>
> *I know your mom and dad relocated for retirement. How are they enjoying their new home?*
>
> *How did you fare in that golf tournament last weekend?*
>
> *What did you think about the Kansas City Chiefs' game on Sunday?*
>
> *Are you planning to run the 10K in Pittsburgh again this year?*

Examples of Email and Text Check-Ins

As we mentioned a little earlier, check-ins can happen in a variety of ways. Here is an example of an email:

> Mark, I hope you're having a great week. I'm excited to hear how your sales calls have been going using the new discovery process. How did the meeting in Dallas go? Were you able to take the prospect out for dinner after the meeting to Bob's Steak & Chop House? Just out of curiosity, how did she like the dinner?

Here is an example of a text:

> You guys have a great day. Heard some decisionmakers are coming. You'll knock it out of the park! Ping me after. Good luck!

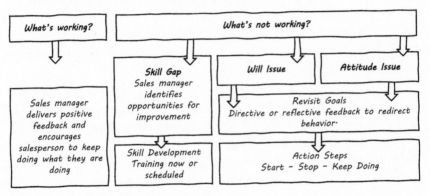

Figure 7.2   Check-In Conversation

As we covered, there are multiple ways to check in with your sales team (i.e. walk-around, email, text, etc.) and there are multiple topics you can check in on (personal, job-related, upcoming events, etc.). What we're going to focus on now is the conversation on what that check-in may look like when it's focused on goals, action steps, and performance.

Once you have transitioned from conversation-starters to deeper questions about what's working/not working, you may uncover a skill gap or a will/attitude issue. If so, you can deliver the appropriate type of feedback that is positive, reflective, or directive. If it is a will or attitude issue, you can revisit goals and set action steps. If it is a skill gap, you can conduct skill development training either just-in-time, or schedule a skill development training session for a later time. Below are some examples of what this might sound like.

Positive Feedback Example – Outbound Sales

Here is an example of positive feedback in an outbound sales setting:

Sales manager: Good afternoon, [Salesperson's name]. I know you set your goal and planned in your schedule to prospect by making 40 calls every day this week. It's Wednesday at 5:00 p.m. How's it going so far this week?

Salesperson: Thanks for dropping by my office. It's only Wednesday and I have already made 160 total calls this week and have set more meetings this week than I ever have in a week. I beat my personal best.

(Salesperson stands up and high-fives sales manager)

Sales manager: That's terrific, [Salesperson's name]! What's working so well for you?

Salesperson: Well for one, I'm really organized with my list of people to call because I created it last Friday before the week ended. This has helped me to make calls in my prospecting time blocks, which has really improved my pace.

Sales manager: Agreed. It sounds like building your list helped you improve your pace. We both know that pace is important. I also want to compliment you on staying inside your time blocks. Doing that every day will achieve all your goals in no time. In our review and plan meeting at the start of the year, I know we discussed one of your goals outside of work was to take your family on vacation to Hawaii this year. Just keep doing what you're doing and the odds of that happening are very high.

Salesperson: That sounds great. Thanks for coming by and checking on my progress.

Sales manager: Are you coming across any challenges?

Salesperson: Just that you're here right now slowing my pace down this morning as I am making my calls. I am just kidding. No real challenges. I'm like butter, I'm on a roll.

Sales manager: I tell you what; if you're salesperson of the month this month, I would love to take you and your spouse out to dinner at a restaurant of your choice.

Salesperson: You're on! My personal favorite is Oki Doki Sushi.

Reflective Feedback Example – Outbound Sales

Sales manager: Good afternoon, [Salesperson's name]. I know you set your goal and planned in your schedule to prospect by making 40 calls every day this week. It's Wednesday at 5:00 p.m. How's it going so far this week?

Salesperson: Alright, I guess. 130 calls so far over the last three days.

Sales manager: 130 calls! You've already exceeded your goal. What's working for you?

Salesperson: I time blocked my call blitzes in my calendar every day for the entire week, which has helped me be disciplined with my pace. I have tried to minimize distractions, then made calls, and never put the phone down.

Sales manager: Nice work. Your discipline is great. I know that staying inside your time blocks is not easy. What's not working for you? Any challenges?

Salesperson: Some of these gatekeepers are tougher than a two-dollar steak. I am having trouble getting through to the decision-maker. I think they all attended some gatekeeper boot camp training down at the Staples Center with Tony Robbins and Malcolm Gladwell teaching them how to screen me out.

Sales manager: I know how difficult it is to work with gatekeepers. I used to be six inches taller before I started in sales. Those gate-keepers have pounded me down into the ground straight up to my armpits. I went all the way from 6'10" to 6'4". What's your opening line?

Salesperson: I have been saying, "Hello, this is [name] with ACME, may I speak to [decision-maker's name] please?"

Sales manager: Are you open to some feedback?

Salesperson: Absolutely, anything would help.

Sales manager: Next time, try changing your opening line by saying this: "Good morning this is [name] with ACME for [decision-maker's name] please."

It's very similar to what you were saying, but instead of asking the gatekeeper for permission, you are more direct in saying your opening line in a way that sounds as if you expect to be passed through. This opening line is so short and easy to practice, why don't we go back and forth ten times right now before you go back to making more calls.

(Sales manager and salesperson go back and forth ten times each, practicing the new opening line)

Salesperson: This is an easy upgrade to make. I'm going to start using it right now. Giddy-up!

Sales manager: Let me know how it goes. A few others have mentioned trouble with gatekeepers too, so we will practice working with them at our next sales meeting.

Directive Feedback Example – Outbound Sales

Sales manager: Good afternoon [Salesperson's name]. I know you set your goal and planned in your schedule to prospect by making 40 calls every day this week. It's Wednesday at 5:00 p.m. How's it going so far this week?

    (Sales manager observes salesperson working furiously on an NCAA basketball pool)

Salesperson: I'm on my way. Already five calls in.

Sales manager: Okay. How did you somehow muscle out those five calls? What's working well for you?

Salesperson: No contacts yet, but I've got a really great list of prospects to call, so I'm looking forward to big results.

Sales manager: I bet you are. The list is important. It's already Wednesday though, and you set the goal in our last goal-setting meeting to make on average at least 40 calls a day. What's getting in your way?

Salesperson: I just need to get more organized because with so much going on right now, I don't really know what to put my attention on.

Sales manager: Yes, I understand it has been busy around here this week. Are you open to some feedback?

Salesperson: Yes.

Sales manager: I am confused because, over the last couple days as I've been walking through the office, I observed you working on your NCAA tournament pool. I was wondering how that is going to contribute to you hitting your goals this week?

Salesperson: Gee, I guess I didn't look at it like that. I need to stick to my plan and get my calls done.

Sales manager: You said it! Why don't you walk me through the action steps that you had planned in our goal-setting meeting and the time blocks you have allocated every day for your call blitzes?

Salesperson: That's a great question. I had set aside two time blocks every day to make calls: in the morning from 9:30 to 11:00 and in the afternoon from 2:00 to 3:30.

Sales manager: Great. My advice to you would be to finish your NCAA pool outside of golden selling time and, over the next two days, I would get as many calls in as I possibly could so I don't throw a bagel on the scoreboard this week. How does that sound?

Salesperson: Sounds like a plan. I'll finish the NCAA pool tonight at home. Then I'll do whatever I can to get as many calls in as possible by the end of the week.

Sales manager: Thanks, [Salesperson's name]. I realize the NCAA pool is a big deal in the office every year. I see how you got caught up in the excitement. Thank you for being open-minded to my feedback and not defensive. I care about you and I want what's best for you.

* * *

Now that we have given a few examples of what a check-in might look like with an outside sales force, let's review some examples that could apply to inbound contact/customer care centers.

Reflective Feedback Example – Inbound Call Center Sales

Sales manager: Hi [Salesperson's name], how is it going with your objection-handling? I noticed your sales conversion has been going up this week – what's been working?

Salesperson: I liked the way, in our last sales meeting, we practiced how to uncover unspoken objections the customer may have, ultimately helping me to isolate what their true objection is that's blocking them from moving forward.

Sales manager: How has that helped you?

Salesperson: Well, you can't resolve the real objection that's blocking them from moving forward if you don't know what it is.

Sales manager: What are you using that we practiced in last week's sales meeting that's working for handling objections?

Salesperson: Whenever I got initial resistance from a customer after I made a recommendation, I used to try to handle the objection. After the training we had in the sales meeting, I have changed my approach. Now, instead of doing that after I get an objection from a customer, I ask a few more questions, such as "What makes you say that? Tell me a little more about your concern" and "Could you be a little more specific?" While they are responding to my questions, I take good notes. After they are done talking, I reflect back to them what I thought I heard in response to my questions by saying something like this, "Thanks for sharing that information with me. It sounds to me that you really like the recommendation, but you're concerned about the cost." They typically respond by saying "Yes." Then I say the magic words that we practiced in our sales meeting which are helping me uncover the hidden concern: "In addition to that, is there anything else that would prevent you from moving forward with what I recommended?" You're never going to believe it, roughly two out of every three times I say that, they give me another objection. Then I ask more questions about that objection and then handle that objection because it's typically the primary objection.

Sales manager: Good for you. Would you mind sharing that success story at our next sales meeting?

Salesperson: Absolutely. I'd be happy to.

Sales manager: Thank you and congratulations on your success! Way to be open-minded to new ideas, practicing those ideas, and implementing those new ideas where it matters most, on calls with our customers. Keep doing what you're doing.

Salesperson: Thanks! I feel like I'm shot out of a cannon right now!

Positive Feedback Example – Inbound Call Center

Sales Manager: Hi [Salesperson's name], how is it going with the close step on your calls today? I remote-monitored you a few times and it sounded really good! You are doing a good job recapping your calls and summarizing next steps.

Salesperson: Thank you!

Sales Manager: What is the impact on your calls?

Salesperson: I can tell the customers are leaving the calls with more confidence.

Sales Manager: Definitely keep doing that because it is working. How open are you to another idea?

Sales manager: Definitely, keep doing that because it's working. How open are you to another idea?

Salesperson: I'm open!

Sales manager: From the calls I've listened to, I've noticed that after you make a recommendation you follow it up with, "Do you have any questions?" From what I observed, it invites a "No" response from your customer. You want to try to avoid asking a question right after you make a recommendation that generates a "No" response from a customer that makes closing the sale more difficult. It can be difficult to turn around a "No." So why create that problem for yourself? How about this, after you make a recommendation, ask the customers, "Have I answered all your questions today?" It doesn't mean that they won't respond with the word "No," but it may improve the probability they will respond with a "Yes" answer. It is a lot easier to ask the customer if they are ready to take the next step after they have said the word "Yes" than after they have said the word "No." It's a minor thing, but we know a little difference makes a big difference in customer satisfaction and net promoter score when you multiply it over thousands of calls.

(Sales manager and salesperson go back and forth, practicing "Have I answered all your questions today?" Until the sales manager thinks the salesperson has done enough quality repetitions that they will replace "Do you have any questions?" with "Have I answered all your questions today?" in their call flow).

Salesperson: Thanks for the feedback. I will use that with my next batch of calls after my break.

Sales manager: Good luck! I'll check back later and see how it is going.

Directive Feedback Example – Inbound Service Center

Sales manager: Hey [Salesperson's name], every time I've stopped by your desk today you haven't been here – what's up?

Salesperson: Well, I had to talk to HR about FMLA, and then I had to talk to workforce management about my schedule. Then I had a question I had to go ask the team lead.

Sales manager: Sounds like you've been busy, all right. Let me ask you, what's the impact on our customers if we're short?

Salesperson: Wait times go up.

Sales manager: How does that impact the team?

Salesperson: From my experience working here, what I have noticed is that the longer a customer is on hold, the more it has a negative impact on their attitude when we talk to them.

Sales manager: I have to agree. So, can you do our customers and the team a favor and try to spread out your off-phone activities a little to make sure the floor is covered?

Salesperson: I can do that.

Sales manager: Thank you!

Regular and consistent conversations are a great way to ensure that your salespeople are working towards the action steps they set in their goal-setting meetings. It also creates an opportunity to check in on other important things such as personal goals and activities your salespeople are doing outside of work. Many salespeople like the follow-up, the attention, the accountability, and the ongoing conversations between goal-setting meetings. It helps them to stay focused and it also gives them opportunities to ask for help. An additional benefit is that you are able to do these check-ins through a wide variety of communication modalities – email, phone call, text, voicemail, drop by the office, conversation in the hallway, etc. These interactions also give you the opportunity to provide positive, reflective, and directive feedback, uncover skill gaps, will/attitude issues, and conduct skill development training to address those opportunities for improvement.

Be somebody who makes everybody feel like a somebody.

—Anonymous

Takeaway Questions

Below are questions you can use for further reflection.

Takeaway Discussion Questions for Your Organization

If you are leading a sales organization, how effective do you think your sales managers are at checking in on a daily,

(continued)

(*continued*)

weekly, or monthly basis with their sales teams to keep the conversations going?

Takeaway Questions for Personal Reflection

If you are leading a sales team, how effective are you at checking in on a daily, weekly, or monthly basis with your sales team to keep the conversations going?

8

Performance Feedback

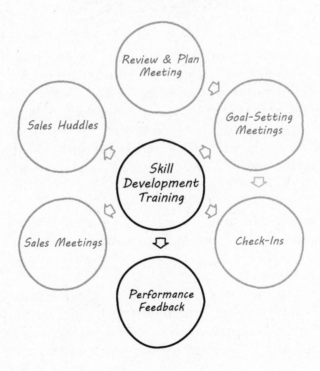

Performance Feedback

Review & Plan Meeting

Goal-Setting Meetings

Sales Huddles

Skill Development Training

Check-Ins

Sales Meetings

Performance Feedback

A COMPETENT SALES MANAGER places more emphasis on preparing their sales team for good performance than they do in the actual performance itself. The way they do this is to have the mindset that they are the practice coach. What happens in the game will be predicated on what happens in practice, because people typically perform like they practice. Many sales managers, unfortunately, do not spend a sufficient amount of time up-front training, coaching, or reinforcing sales skills with their team prior to live engagement with prospects or customers. As a result, their activity is limited to observing their sales team in action and the performance they see will probably be in direct correlation to the amount of practice and preparation that preceded the actual performance. In this context, they are merely the game coach. The ideal is to be both the practice coach and the game coach.

> *Practice like you've never won. Play like you've never lost.*
> —Michael Jordan

The Practice Coach, the Game Coach, Then the Practice Coach

The practice coach spends a lot of time doing dry runs, dress rehearsals, and skill development training to help their salespeople develop the abilities to have an impact in the game. The practice coach knows that their job is to develop their team and it will require a tremendous investment in time, energy, and effort. They also know that the outcome of any competition is generally determined by the level of practice beforehand. The practice coach knows that it will often be boring. It is repetitive. It is not glamorous.

> If the activities that lead to greatness were easy and fun, then everyone would do them and they would not distinguish the best from the rest. (Colvin 2010, 72)

In a sales culture, it is critical to have systems in place that continually improve your sales team's performance. Delivering consistent performance feedback is one of those systems, because it creates consistency in approach and methodology across your sales team. It helps you

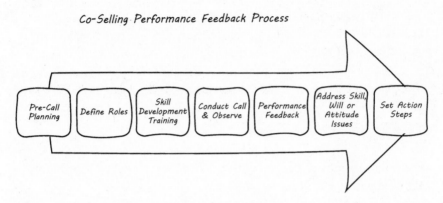

Figure 8.1   Co-Selling Performance Feedback

to see in real time a salesperson's strengths and weaknesses and gives you the opportunity to deliver feedback when it matters most, right after a selling interaction.

Keep in mind that, to make this happen, you want to plan adequate time for delivering performance feedback after the meeting/call and consider the setting in which it will occur. For example, if you are in outside sales, you could meet your salesperson for breakfast and prepare and practice before the meeting. Then, after the meeting, you could get into the car and deliver performance feedback there; or, you may decide to go to a coffee shop. You may also meet at the office prior to the meeting to prepare and practice and then return to the office to deliver performance feedback. If you are in a contact center, you could meet in a conference room to prepare and practice. Then, you could sit deskside with your salesperson and return to the conference room to deliver performance feedback. The main thing is to ensure you have the proper time allotted and the right setting for the debrief.

Define Roles and Responsibilities

In this time together you will typically be in one of three roles as the sales manager – leader, co-seller, or observer. The role and responsibility you define will be specific and relevant to the salesperson you are working with and the situation you are in. One way to ensure that

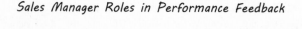

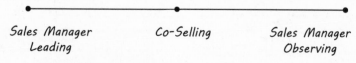

Figure 8.2   Sales Manager Roles

your salesperson will succeed with performance feedback is by being an effective practice coach.

The Leader

Let's address the first role you could be in, which is the leader. In this role, you will be the one conducting the call/meeting and your salesperson will be solely in the observation role. This approach is particularly beneficial for brand new salespeople, experienced salespeople who are new to your team, or other salespeople on your team whom you feel would benefit from seeing you in action. Believe it or not, there are still a percentage of experienced, successful salespeople who respect you and would love to see how you do it. Prior to taking the lead in any meeting/call, you will set aside ample time to get together with your salesperson to prepare and practice for the meeting/call. Many sales managers don't do this. Oftentimes they are checking their phone, returning emails, or sending text messages when they should be fully present preparing and practicing for the meeting/call.

To prepare, you and your salesperson will discuss the strategy and goals for what you want to accomplish in the meeting/call together. You will **explain** how you will use the company's defined sales process and methodology to help achieve the desired outcome. You will have the one-page call flow/template with you and provide a copy for your salesperson. As the leader, you will then use the call flow/template to **demonstrate** how to prepare for, and then **practice** conducting the meeting/call with the salesperson in the role of prospect/customer. Then, you will reverse roles and your salesperson will **practice** conducting the meeting/call as the leader, mirroring your demonstration. You will be in the role of prospect/customer as your salesperson practices. Time permitting, you should do this multiple times. That is what the practice coach is all about. While you are practicing together, you will **observe** their practice and give them **feedback**. Even though you will be leading the meeting/call, you will still be the practice coach before the meeting/call starts. This technique of using your company's sales process and methodology will create consistency and uniformity in your sales team's approach.

Then, you will conduct the meeting/call together with you leading the meeting, exemplifying all the right behaviors. Your salesperson can learn by observing what success looks like using your company's sales process and methodology.

A few challenges to be aware of as the leader:

- You might like doing this so much that, in later co-selling situations, you may find it hard to relinquish control.
- If you are not the practice coach before and after you lead the meeting or call, your sales team may become overly dependent on you to close all their deals because they are not developing their own skills.
- You may be developing the relationship with the customer instead of your salesperson. You can't be the single point of contact for every customer.

> *A leader is one who knows the way, goes the way, and shows the way.*
>
> —John C. Maxwell

The Observer

At the other end of the spectrum, the salesperson takes the lead in the meeting/call. Your role in the meeting is to observe, take notes, and deliver performance feedback after the meeting. This approach is more suited when working with a salesperson who is more tenured, experienced, and successful. This is the end zone for where you want to be as a sales manager. When you have reached this level, it means that all of the repetitive skill development and practice sessions have worked. All you need to do now is watch the game and give feedback.

However, you will still follow the same process that you followed when you were the leader in the meeting/call.

Prior to being the observer in any meeting/call, you will do the same thing you would do if you were the leader: set aside ample time to get together with your salesperson to prepare and practice for the meeting/call.

To prepare, you and your salesperson will discuss the strategy and goals for what you want to accomplish in the meeting/call together. You will **explain** how you will use the company's defined sales process and methodology to help achieve the desired outcome. You will have the one-page call flow/template with you and provide a copy for your salesperson. You will then use the call flow/template to **demonstrate** how to prepare for and **practice** conducting the meeting/call with the salesperson in the role of prospect/customer. Then, you will reverse roles and your salesperson will **practice** conducting the meeting as the leader, modeling your demonstration. You will be in the role of prospect/customer as your salesperson practices. Time permitting, you should do this multiple times. That is what the practice coach is all about. While you are practicing together, you will **observe** their practice and give them **feedback**. Even though they will be leading the meeting/call, you will still be the practice coach before the meeting/call starts. The only thing that is different between you being the leader or the observer is that the salesperson conducts the meeting/call, not you. The strategizing, planning, and practice is the same regardless of your role in the meeting/call. You will conduct the meeting/call together with your salesperson leading the meeting/call, doing what they practiced prior to the meeting/call. You will observe and take notes. After the meeting, you will deliver performance feedback.

> *Master the art of observing.*
>
> —Anonymous

The Co-Seller

There are a variety of situations when you are with your sales team and you will be co-selling together. Prior to the meeting/call, when you co-sell, you will identify roles and responsibilities for what each of you will do in the meeting/call. Here are just a few examples of when co-selling would be beneficial:

- Your salesperson is less experienced, and you have been leading their meetings/calls as they go through training. Now it's time to begin to transition some of the responsibilities over to the salesperson in a safe environment. If things do not go as planned, you're still there to support them. If things do go well, it will build their confidence in their ability to conduct meetings/calls on their own. If they perform poorly, you will be able to observe what they did that did not work and you will be there to help them salvage the opportunity by supporting them in the meeting. After the meeting you will know precisely where the opportunity for improvement is and you can roll right into skill development training to address the gap.
- This is a big opportunity and your salesperson wants to demonstrate to the prospect/customer that there is more than one person representing your company, they are part of a team.
- Your salesperson knows the prospect/customer wants to know that they are part of a team, which can deliver on expectations.
- Your salesperson asks you to be with them because they know there will be multiple decision-makers in the room, and they want your support.
- You feel the different experiences and expertise that you each bring to the table would add value to the prospect/customer in that meeting/call.
- You are acclimating a new salesperson to an account or sales territory.

When co-selling, remember to remind yourself of the goal you are trying to achieve in the meeting/call and the roles and responsibilities you have defined for you and your salesperson to achieve that goal. Unfortunately, many sales managers lose sight of the goal and fall back on doing what they do best, which is selling. This could achieve the goal in the short term but do more harm in the long term. For example:

- This could diminish the value of the salesperson in the eyes of the prospect/customer.

- It could negatively impact their salesperson's self-confidence.
- It could create a dynamic where the prospect/customer would rather deal with the sales manager than the salesperson.
- It could inhibit their ability to build their skills. Sometimes a salesperson can learn more from their own mistakes than they do from observing the successes of others.
- It could build resentment towards each other.

Prior to co-selling in any meeting/call, you will do the same thing you would do if you were the leader or observer: set aside ample time to get together with your salesperson to prepare and practice for the meeting/call.

> For the strength of the pack is the wolf, and the strength of the wolf is the pack.
>
> —Rudyard Kipling

Performance Feedback Process

There is more to delivering performance feedback than many sales managers think. Less is more. Fewer calls and meetings can actually add up to more when you're working together. More time to practice before the call, more time to deliver performance feedback after the meeting/call, and more time to address skill gaps and attitude issues after the meeting. Regardless of your role in the meeting, leader, observer, or co-seller, you will still go through the steps above.

Outside Sales

In outside sales, it is very common for you and your salesperson to spend a day or half a day together going on meetings/calls. It would be great if you could have the day jam-packed full of meetings/calls for you both to go to together, but it may not be the best way to help the salesperson develop their skills. For example, it might be better to go on three meetings together in one day as opposed to six. If you went on three meetings, it could probably enable you to implement the seven-step process for delivering performance feedback. If you went on

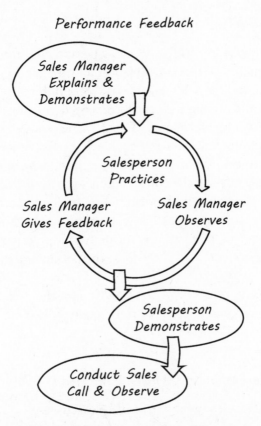

Performance Feedback

Figure 8.3   Delivering Performance Feedback Process

six meetings, it could dramatically reduce the probability that you will have the time to be the practice coach. It could increase the probability that you would take over the meeting/call. It will limit your ability to deliver feedback and address any skill gaps and/or will/attitude issues.

Contact Centers

In a contact center environment, the same principle applies. You don't need to listen to 20 recorded calls or sit deskside for 90 minutes. If you listen to one recorded call or observe one live call and identify an opportunity for improvement, you're ready to implement the process above (or, you could coach proactively without any call observation, as we discuss in Chapter 11).

Performance Feedback Form

Two things happen in a well-conducted performance feedback session. One is the quality of the conversation and interaction between the sales manager and the salesperson. The second thing is how well that conversation and interaction gets documented. Because of this, we recommend you use a performance feedback form that will help guide the conversation in the meeting and enable you to document the conversation. Keep in mind that the most important thing when delivering performance feedback is the conversation – you are only using the form to document the conversation. So, we are going to introduce you to a delivering performance feedback template we have used with our clients as a starting point that you can customize to your sales team. We strongly recommend that you keep the performance feedback form to one page.

Now let's look at how you might use the template to help guide the flow of the conversation when delivering performance feedback.

Delivering Performance Feedback Conversation Flow

Step 1: Overview what you will be discussing
- Review what the salesperson felt they did well.
- Review what the salesperson felt were opportunities for improvement.
- Sales manager reviews observations of what went well.
- Sales manager reviews observations of opportunities for improvement.
- Gain agreement on opportunities for improvement (skill/attitude).
- Sales manager addresses the opportunity for improvement.

Step 2: Discovery – sales manager asks salesperson questions
- What they did well.
- What they felt were opportunities for improvement.

Step 3: Sales manager reviews their observations and gains agreement

Performance Feedback

Name   Date

Account Executive: What Went Well (strengths)		
Account Executive: Opportunities for Improvement		
Sales Manager: What Went Well (strengths)		
Sales Manager: Opportunities for Improvement		
Skills Gaps	Skills Trained	Other Behaviors
Action Steps		

_____   _____
Account Executive Signature   Sales Manager Signature

Figure 8.4   Performance Feedback Form

o What the salesperson did well.

o What they felt were opportunities for improvement for the salesperson.

o Summarize conversation.

o Gain agreement on opportunities for improvement.

Step 4: Address the opportunities for improvement

o Skill gap – skill development training.

o Attitude issue – conversation.

Step 5: Set action steps

o Agree upon action steps.

o Sign and date the form.

o Give encouragement.

Step 1: Overview What You Will Be Discussing

You will begin delivering performance feedback by giving your salesperson a quick overview of what you will be discussing as you deliver feedback. The first couple of times you do this, you will probably need to show your salesperson the form and overview it as you are using it to guide and document the conversation. Using the form will help you keep your feedback session on track and ensure you cover all the important topics.

Sales manager: [Salesperson's name], that was a great meeting. I really appreciate you asking me to come along with you today. Now that the meeting is over, I think it's a great opportunity to discuss what you felt you did well in the meeting and any opportunities for improvement. Then I'll share my observations with you of what I felt you did well and any opportunities for improvement. Then I'll summarize what we discussed, and we can come to an agreement on what you did well and what the opportunities for improvement are. If there is a skill gap, we will address it right now. Since it just happened, we're better able to specifically target and fix what didn't go well while it's fresh in our minds. If there are any other opportunities for improvement, we can discuss them also. We'll conclude by summarizing and setting action steps. How does that sound?

Account Executive: What Went Well (strengths)

Having a printed agenda for the meeting went great. Prospect really liked it. We allocated 90 minutes for the meeting but were able to cover all the points in the agenda in 60 minutes so everybody was happy that they got back 30 minutes of time in their day. Saw them taking notes on the meeting agenda which I thought was a good sign. We really practiced the value proposition before the meeting and that helped me be more comfortable and confident when I was presenting it to the prospect.

Account Executive: Opportunities for Improvement

I noticed that when I was asking questions, I would ask a really good question and they would come back with an answer and I felt I could have dug a little deeper into understanding why they said what they said. I could have also asked more questions than I did to gain a better understanding of their situation. I felt when they were answering my questions I just wanted to jump in and offer a solution. I need to slow down and be more methodical with my discovery questions.

Figure 8.5   Performance Feedback Form Salesperson

As you think about how you are going to overview the conversation when delivering performance feedback, one important point you want to make is that, after you agree that there is a skill gap, you will address it immediately with skill development training. Practicing after performance might be the best time to practice. At this moment, practicing is probably the last thing you want to do, but might be the most important thing you can do.

Step 2: Discovery – Sales Manager Asks Salesperson Questions

After you have outlined what you will be doing, it's time to get going. The best way to start is by asking questions. Just like in the goal-setting meeting, when you started by reviewing their biggest victory first to begin on a positive note, you will apply the same concept here by asking them what they felt they did well in the meeting – a great way to identify, focus, and build on their strengths. After you have had a discussion on what went well, you will shift gears and ask if they feel there were any opportunities for improvement. While you are asking questions and listening, you will be taking notes in the appropriate box on the form.

Sales manager: [Salesperson's name], let's get right to it. What do you think you did well in the meeting?

(Salesperson responds)

Sales manager: What makes you say that?
  (Salesperson responds)
Sales manager: Agreed. In addition to that, is there anything else you think you did well today?
  (Salesperson responds)
Sales manager: Tell me more about that.
  (Salesperson responds)
Sales manager: Thanks for sharing your thoughts with me. Seems like you are pretty tuned in with what you did well in that meeting.
  (Salesperson responds)
Sales manager: What did you think were some of the opportunities for improvement?
  (Salesperson responds)
Sales manager: What makes you say that?
  (Salesperson responds)

As you are asking your salesperson what went well and they respond, you want to ask additional clarifying questions to encourage them to provide specific details that support what they said. Likewise, when you ask them what their opportunities for improvement are, you will ask clarifying questions, encouraging them to give you the specifics about why they think it's an opportunity for improvement. In our example, the two questions we used to help them explain their responses in more detail are: "What makes you say that?" and "Tell me more about that." There are others but these are just two examples.

Telling creates resistance. Asking creates relationships.

—Andrew Sobel

Sales Manager: What Went Well (strengths)

Set a great agenda – conversational, prospect liked the flow.
Well-delivered value proposition – prospect felt you were credible working with companies just like theirs.

Sales Manager: Opportunities for Improvement

Ask more questions. Dig deeper. What do they really mean by what they're saying?

Figure 8.6   Performance Feedback Form Sales Manager

Step 3: Sales Manager Reviews Their Observations and Gains Agreement

After you have asked your salesperson what they thought they did well and what their opportunities for improvement were in the meeting/call, you confirmed understanding by reflecting back what they said. Now, you will transition into sharing your observations of what they did well (strengths) and any opportunities for improvement. Notice in the following example, when you are communicating your observations for what they did well and the opportunities for improvement, you will support your feedback with specific details. Note the bridging phrase in each scenario, **"The reason I say that is because ... "** This bridging phrase is important when delivering performance feedback because it connects the feedback you are giving them with the observable behavior that produced the outcome. In many cases, sales managers take a broad-brush approach in delivering feedback. It is not supported with real specifics based on the behaviors they observed. Here is an example of an effective coaching dialogue:

Sales manager: Thanks for sharing that information with me. Let me give you some feedback on what I thought you did well and any opportunities for improvement I observed.

First of all, I agree with what you said about setting the agenda and delivering your value proposition. I thought you did a good job on both of those. The reason I say that is because, when you overviewed the printed agenda with the prospect in a very conversational manner, they got an understanding of what was going to happen, became very relaxed, and were really open to following the flow of what you laid out in the agenda. Then, when you asked them if there was anything else they would like to add to the agenda, they looked at each other and appeared to gain a consensus that you had a solid agenda for the meeting, and they had nothing else to add.

Secondarily, when you communicated your value proposition, you really gave them a clear overview of what we do, how we do it, who we do it for that is similar to them, and how our clients benefit from what we do. The reason I say that is because, when you were overviewing the type of clients we work with that are just like them, I could sense a greater connection between you and them developing because they felt you were credible and experienced in working with companies that are similar to them. That was not a generic value proposition. You took the time to think it through and made it very specific to them, which I believe lowered their resistance to you and, as a result, they were very forthcoming with information while you were asking questions.

In addition to those two points, one other thing I thought you did well was how you set next steps moving forward. The reason I say that is because, before we walked out of the meeting, you already had your date and time set for the next meeting and you were very clear on the purpose of that meeting. Nice job in there. What are your thoughts on the feedback I gave you?

(Salesperson responds)

Sales manager: Now, let's discuss some opportunities for improvement. There are a couple things I noticed.

One thing I noticed was, after you overviewed our fee structure with the prospect and they began asking questions about the overall cost, it felt to me like you took their questions personally, got frustrated and came off a little defensive. The reason I say that is because I noticed your demeanor immediately changed in the meeting when they started asking questions about our fees. Fortunately, you self-corrected relatively quickly so that it did not impact the outcome of the meeting. What are your thoughts on that?

(Salesperson responds)

Sales manager: Tell me more.

(Salesperson responds)

Sales manager: I understand why you feel the way you do. I understand you were caught off guard with their questions. When those situations come up again in future meetings, what will you do differently?

(Salesperson responds with a good idea)

Sales manager: Great idea. One thing that I've learned over time is that after I have made a recommendation, I will probably get the same questions, concerns, or resistance time after time. As a result, before I go into any meeting where I know I will be presenting a proposal, I mentally prepare myself before the meeting. The way I do that is I formulate some questions I can ask when they come up and prepare talking points to use to address those concerns. This level of preparation helps me to not take these objections so personally and not be defensive in these situations. Over time, I've come to realize they are not criticizing me, they are just asking questions about the fees. I don't think it really affected the outcome of the meeting because you got the next meeting on the calendar, which was the goal. Here's what I'd suggest. Prior to your next meeting, let's get together, look at the proposal you're recommending, anticipate some of the concerns that may arise after you present your recommendation, and practice how to address those concerns. How does that sound?

(Salesperson responds)

Sales manager: The other thing I noticed is what you mentioned, asking better discovery questions. The reason I say that is because I think you had a really good initial question but when they responded with their answer I felt you could have asked another question that would have enabled the prospect to give you more clarity around what they meant by what they said. For example, when you asked them, "What's important to you in a relationship with a partner?" They responded with, "We want good service." You could have dug a little deeper by asking more questions. In the future when someone says, "We want good service," what question could you ask?

Salesperson: What is your definition of good service? If good service were happening, what would that look like?

Sales manager: That's great. I think that would be a good upgrade moving forward when you are asking questions.

When feedback on what went well is supported with specifics, the salesperson gains confidence and is more likely to repeat the behavior that worked. Over time, that behavior will become a strength and in turn, become a good habit. When feedback on the opportunity for improvement is supported with specifics, the salesperson has a crystal-clear picture of what did not work and can make necessary

Skills Gaps	Skills Trained	Other Behaviors
Asking more questions	Discovery questions	Avoid getting defensive when objections occur

Figure 8.7   Performance Feedback Form Skill Development

adjustments to their approach to generate better results in the future, thus turning their opportunities for improvement into strengths and cultivating better habits.

Step 4: Address the Opportunities for Improvement

Any sales manager can ask their salesperson what went well and what they could have done better. Then they agree – that's where the conversation typically ends. Then they both sit there and admire the problem. "Wow, we both agreed that you could have done better at asking questions." Nothing comes after that. There is no real effort to close that skill gap immediately. But it's not going to go away or improve without it being addressed through practice. You talk about the problem, agree on the problem, yet do nothing to solve the problem. Really? I mean, really? So, why is that?

One reason is poor planning. You did not schedule enough time in the day to be the practice coach, the game coach, and then the practice coach. You have to prepare and practice up-front, identify roles and responsibilities, conduct the meeting/call, and then leave enough time to deliver feedback and conduct a skill development training session.

The second reason is because the problem shows up on your front porch, dressed in a pair of overalls, and it's called "work." In an ideal world, you were the practice coach, then the game coach, and, now that the game is over, you're tired and don't want to be the practice coach again. We don't want to hurt your feelings, but there is a high degree of probability that you weren't the practice coach before the game even started! Now that the meeting/call is over, the investment required to be the practice coach again and dive into a 15 to 30-minute skill development training session can be very unappealing.

Another reason the skill gap isn't addressed immediately after the meeting/call is that you're just ready to get on with your day, get back to the office, return emails, get to the airport, get to the next meeting, etc. This meeting is over and you're ready to get on with what's next.

Finally, another reason you may be reluctant to dive into a skill development session is that you feel the salesperson will be resistant to the training. Let's say the meeting/call didn't go that well and you know your salesperson is disappointed in the outcome. It might appear to you that they are not in the right frame of mind to be open to feedback, let alone a 15 to 30-minute skill development session.

> *In the middle of every difficulty lies opportunity.*
> —Albert Einstein

Here is an example of what it could sound like to transition into a skill development session:

Sales manager: [Salesperson's name], looks like we agree you could have been more effective in the meeting/call by digging a little deeper with your questions. While we're here right now and it's fresh in our minds, there is no time like the present to take advantage of the opportunity to practice asking questions and digging deeper. What we're going to work on is asking questions. Why this is important to you is because it will help you further develop your ability to ask a question, and allow the prospect to respond to the question and ask a clarifying question to gather additional information. Here is how we're going to do it. First, I am going to explain how to peel back the onion through questioning. Then, I will demonstrate what it might sound like. Then, we will practice – I will go and then you will go. We will go back and forth until you feel confident in your ability to drill down deeper with your discovery questions. I'll observe you and give you feedback as you practice to help you get better, faster. When we're done, you will have the opportunity to give me a demonstration of what we worked on to make sure that you got it. How does that sound?

Ideally, you will now have completed the cycle, which is the vision of what you want to accomplish when you invest your time with your salesperson by delivering performance feedback, which is to be the practice coach, the game coach, and then the practice coach again. Now it's time to set next steps moving forward.

Step 5: Set Action Steps

You have just completed a skill development session to address a skill gap and possibly had a conversation to address an attitude issue, which you saw in the example. Now it's time to put some action steps in place moving forward and give your salesperson encouragement that, if they implement the improvements you discussed and practiced, they should be able to get better results the next time they are in a similar situation. Here is an example dialogue:

Sales manager: [Salesperson's name], it was nice to spend time in the field with you today. Thanks a lot for setting up some great meetings. I look forward to doing this with you again next month. In our last meeting of the day I thought you did some things really well, in particular how you set the agenda and presented your value proposition. I also want to compliment you on your ability to self-identify some of your opportunities for improvement with your mindset for how to react when you get an objection about the cost, and in your ability to ask more clarifying questions. I also appreciated that when the meeting was over and we debriefed, we were able to have a conversation about having the right attitude when handling objections, and then we moved right into a practice session about how to dig deeper in asking questions. What's one action step you want to take coming out of the time we spent together today?

Salesperson: Before my next meeting, I am going to go through my discovery meeting template and practice my questions so that when I get into the meeting, I will be more effective with the drill-down questions. I will also anticipate any potential questions or concerns they may have about our cost structure and I will be better mentally prepared to address those concerns should they come up.

Sales manager: Fantastic. What I'm going to do is I'm going to check in with you after your next meeting and we can discuss how it went. Let's both sign and date the form so we both have a record of what we did today. Good luck on your next meeting. I know that you

Performance Feedback

Name Mark Norman   **Date** 7/1

Account Executive: What Went Well (strengths)
Having a printed agenda for the meeting went great. Prospect really liked it. We allocated 90 minutes for the meeting but were able to cover all the points in the agenda in 60 minutes, so everybody was happy that they got back 30 minutes of time in their day. Saw them taking notes on the meeting agenda which I thought was a good sign. We really practiced the value proposition before the meeting and that helped me be more comfortable and confident when I was presenting it to the prospect.
Account Executive: Opportunities for Improvement
I noticed that when I was asking questions, I would ask a really good question and they would come back with an answer and I felt I could have dug a little deeper into understanding why they said what they said. I could have also asked more questions than I did to gain a better understanding of their situation. I felt when they were answering my questions I just wanted to jump in and offer a solution. I need to slow down and be more methodical with my discovery questions.
Sales Manager: What Went Well (strengths)
Set a great agenda – conversational, prospect liked the flow. Well-delivered value proposition – prospect felt you were credible working with companies just like theirs.
Sales Manager: Opportunities for Improvement
Ask more questions. Dig deeper. What do they really mean by what they're saying?

Skills Gaps	Skills Trained	Other Behaviors
Asking more questions	Discovery questions	Avoid getting defensive when objections occur

Action Steps
Practice discovery questions from template; mentally prepare for objections

Mark Norman   Steve Johnson
_____   _____
Account Executive Signature   **Sales Manager Signature**

Figure 8.8   Performance Feedback Form Signed

will be able to implement the things we worked on today. Go get 'em tiger!!! ROAR!

> *The way to get started is to quit talking and begin doing.*
> —Walt Disney

After you have agreed on the action steps and signed and dated the form, you want to provide encouragement to your salesperson. Let them know that you are behind them 100% and you are confident they are on the right track.

Insights on Performance Feedback

We have tried to paint a picture for you of what performance feedback could potentially look like: defining roles of leader, co-selling, observer; being the practice coach, the game coach, then the practice coach again; having a meaningful debrief after the meeting/call is over; documenting that conversation; rolling right into a conversation about attitude or addressing a skill gap with some training.

In reality, many sales managers do not deliver performance feedback. If they do, the frequency of doing it can be very inconsistent. Many times, they only do it when there is a glaring performance issue that needs to be addressed. When they do it, the greatest percentage of the time, they are just the game coach. There is very little, if any, practice up-front and very little practice after. Therefore, the time they spend with their salespeople has very little impact on performance.

It is also important to be aware that many salespeople do not like or are uncomfortable in these types of situations. Here are a few reasons why:

- They feel, when they are with their sales manager, that they are put on the spot, under a microscope, and it's uncomfortable.
- If their sales performance is mediocre, they are concerned about their sales manager seeing them in action.
- They have their own way of doing things and don't respond well to receiving that type of feedback.

- They think they know it all, better than the sales manager, and having the sales manager with them adds no value and could even hinder their performance.
- They're concerned their sales manager may see that they have not been doing their job.
- They don't want their sales manager along because the sales manager's style, personality, and demeanor are dominating and tend to take over, diminishing the salesperson's relationship with the customer/prospect.

Not all salespeople feel that way. Some really enjoy spending time with their sales manager, working together. Here are some of the reasons why:

- Sales can be a very lonely job. When they have their sales manager with them, not only do they have the opportunity to get better, but they enjoy the partnership.
- They like the face time, attention, and support from their sales manager.
- They feel that their sales manager is invested not only in their job, but in their career path as well.
- Some salespeople who are accustomed to getting feedback really like getting it because it helps them get better.
- When their sales manager is really good at what they do, the salesperson feels they can learn from them. The sales manager can help them land opportunities. It gives them something to emulate.

Let's review the big picture. You have done a review and plan, you are conducting consistent goal-setting meetings, and you're checking in between those meetings on a formal and informal basis to keep the conversation going. You're doing a great job. Of all the activities we have covered so far in this book, from our experience the one that has the lowest level of execution is delivering performance feedback. So, the question we have for you is, how do you ever really improve your salesperson's skills and abilities if you don't see them in action?

Why is delivering performance feedback so poorly executed? It takes big chunks of time. It gets nudged out by the tyranny of the day.

It's important but not urgent so it tends to get put off and rescheduled. You want to talk about employee engagement? Give your salespeople the gift of your full attention and invest your time in them while they are doing their job. Some sales organizations are so serious about delivering performance feedback that they create a certification or evaluation process. That process is anchored to the sales process and methodology of the organization. When the sales manager is delivering performance feedback, the sales process and methodology is the benchmark for the feedback that is delivered. The act of doing this is one of the most important activities you can do to optimize the investment your organization has made in sales training – to be with your salespeople to observe how they are implementing the training on the job and to see what types of results they are getting.

> *The key to learning is feedback. It is nearly impossible to learn any-thing without it.*
>
> —Steven Levitt

Takeaway Questions

Below are questions you can use for further reflection.

Takeaway Discussion Questions for Your Organization

- If you are leading a sales organization, how effective do you think your sales managers are in delivering performance feed-back with the salespeople on their team?
- What is the opportunity for improvement?

Takeaway Questions for Personal Reflection

- If you are leading a sales team, how effective are you at delivering performance feedback with the salespeople on your team?
- What is your opportunity for improvement?

9

Sales Meetings

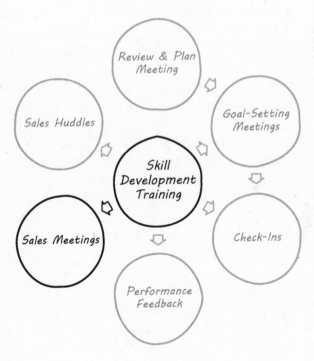

Sales Meetings

Much has been written about the cost of unproductive meetings (Perlow, Hadley, and Eun 2017). For example, let's assume that you have a weekly, 1-hour sales meeting with 10 people on your team, and they make an average of $150,000 each per year. The cost of that 1-hour meeting is $1,050. If you were to have 50 of those per year, the average annual cost of your sales meetings would be $50,250. The questions you want to ask yourself are: "Are my sales meetings productive? Are they worth the time my salespeople are out of the field/off the phones engaged in a non-revenue generating activity?" If you answered "No" to one or both questions, then be glad you have this book in your hands right now because we have gathered best practices from over 2,500 sales managers on how they conduct productive sales meetings. What's in this chapter could add some potential value to your sales organization and your sales team.

What we're going to do in this chapter is to share with you a proven sales meeting process because we believe that there are certain elements that every sales meeting should have. We realize you need to mix it up from time to time and we're going to give you some ideas and best practices of other activities you can weave into the sales meeting process we are providing. You can bring these activities into your sales meetings when needed, without breaking away from your sales meeting process.

A sales meeting is a tremendous opportunity for you to focus your sales team, build their confidence, and conduct skill development training. You can turn sales meetings into productive time if you understand how to prepare for, facilitate, and sequence the events in the meeting. Sales is a job that requires tremendous motivation and enthusiasm. You must think in terms of turning your sales meeting into an opportunity to energize, focus, and inspire your sales team.

> *Enthusiasm is the yeast that rises the dough.*
>
> —Paul J. Meyer

Earlier in the book we discussed the benefits of having a repeatable process for your sales meetings that you can customize. It also makes sense for you to conduct your sales meetings on a consistent basis. You will determine the frequency that is best for your team, such as weekly, bi-weekly, or monthly, at the same time, on the same day of the week (e.g. the second Monday of the month at 8:00 a.m.). This will enable your sales team to get into a routine and form the habit of blocking off time and attending meetings consistently. By having the same sales meeting process and conducting the meetings with consistent frequency, your chances of conducting productive sales meetings will increase. Here's why: your sales team will know exactly when the meeting will be held, day of the week and time, and what's going to happen when they get there. As a result, attendance, participation, and engagement will improve.

What you don't want to do is repeatedly change the day/time of your sales meeting to fit around your schedule. You will be sending a message to your team that the meeting isn't important and that your time is more important than theirs.

Based on our experience in partnering with our clients, we have developed a framework that has the important elements of an effective sales meeting. Now, let's overview a sales meeting process based on that framework which could serve as a roadmap for you. We will lay out what the process looks like based on a sales meeting agenda. Then we will break it down one step at a time and show you exactly how to conduct the meeting following the process. After that, we will touch on a variety of other activities you can move in and out of this sales meeting process when necessary.

Top Ten Reasons Why Salespeople Hate Sales Meetings

Just for the heck of it, let's overview why salespeople do not like to take time out of their day, week, or month to attend unproductive sales meetings, keeping in mind that we could probably write an entire book on this topic. We'll try to keep it brief. While you read through these 10 reasons, please circle or highlight the ones that resonate with you. Here we go.

1. The meeting is for the sake of having a meeting. There is no clear objective or goal.
2. The meetings don't start on time, don't end on time, and run too long.

3. The meeting doesn't start on a positive note or end on a positive note; nor does it follow any sort of agenda. There is no consistent process or flow to the meeting.

4. It's not really a sales meeting, it's an operations meeting, status update, gripe session, and the sales manager talks the whole time.

5. Best practices, success stories, and new ideas are not shared.

6. There is no training, interactivity, or participation on the part of the sales team in the meeting. They don't learn anything new or reinforce existing skills.

7. There is very little recognition or praise given to members of the sales team to acknowledge their performance.

8. The tone of the meeting is negative. The team leaves feeling like they have had a good old-fashioned ass-whoopin'. It's a sales beating, not a sales meeting.

9. The meetings are boring. The meetings are boring. The meetings are boring.

10. As a result of the nine reasons above, salespeople show up to the meeting with a bad attitude. They would rather be out selling, making money, than sitting in the conference room, warming up a chair, trying to stay awake and checking their phone under the table, hoping the sales manager doesn't notice.

You have probably not had anything as ridiculous as any of these 10 things occur with your sales meetings. But, on the odd chance that you have, which of these 10 reasons resonated with you and why?

Sales Meeting Agenda

As you look at the sales meeting agenda below, you will notice that it is scheduled for 1 hour. We recommend that your sales meetings last no more than 1 hour because some salespeople tend to have limited attention spans. In conducting thousands of live and virtual sales meetings/training sessions, we have found that our observations on participants' attention spans are in line with the Pareto principle, the 80/20 rule. About 80% of your salespeople will stay engaged for 30 minutes. At 40 minutes, it drops to 60%. At 50 minutes, it drops to 40%. It continues to go downhill from there. If you have a large team, you may need the entire hour. If you have a smaller sales team that is very experienced, you may be able to conduct this meeting in 45 minutes. You will still use the same process and sequence, but you will adapt how much time you allocate to each topic. So, here is what the meeting agenda could look like:

Sales Meeting Agenda

Sales Meeting Agenda	*Large Conference Room*	*Monday, Jan 27 8:00-9:00 a.m.*
Topic	*Minutes Allotted*	*Cumulative Time*
Welcome	2	*8:02*
Opening Inspiration	5	*8:07*
Success Stories	15	*8:22*
Skill Development Training	15	*8:37*
Goal Reporting & Setting	15	*8:52*
Summary & Action Steps	3	*8:55*
Next Meeting	2	*8:57*
Closing Inspiration	3	*9:00*

Figure 9.1   Sales Meeting Agenda

A best practice is to share the agenda with your sales team prior to the meeting. This will enable them to understand what is going to happen and prepare for the meeting. When salespeople know what to expect, they will be better prepared when they come to the meeting, which will increase the efficiency of the meeting, reducing the amount of time to conduct the meeting and improving the productivity of the meeting.

The End Game

Over time, your team will adjust and get comfortable with the format of the sales meeting. Once that has happened, the next step is to begin to coach and train members of your sales team to take a leadership role for conducting specific activities in the sales meeting. You will be grooming them as peer-to-peer coaches and/or potential future sales leaders in the company. They benefit by developing their skills and abilities in conducting sales meetings, which could positively impact their career path.

Once you have developed a few peer-to-peer coaches on your team, you can then begin to rotate responsibility for the sales meeting to different salespeople on the team. At some point, it is very common for somebody on your sales team to conduct the entire meeting on their own. You can then begin to rotate the responsibility for conducting the entire sales meeting among the members of your sales team. When you do this, an amazing transformation will occur in your sales meetings. When they are running the sales meetings with and for each other, their attention, buy-in, and engagement will dramatically increase the productivity of the sales meetings. The reason is that the quality of a sales meeting is in direct correlation with the quality of the participation in the meeting.

Anchoring back to Chapter 8, where we discussed the role of the practice coach, the game coach, and then the practice coach, you will ultimately follow the same exact process in coaching and training your salespeople in the sales meetings. Once you have this process embedded, you will focus your time and energy on practicing with your salespeople how to conduct elements of the meeting. You will then observe them conducting the sales meeting. When the meeting is over, you will deliver performance feedback and, once again, you will be the practice coach. Imagine a world where your salespeople are conducting all of your sales meetings and are supportive, cooperative, respectful, and encouraging each other in their efforts.

We just wanted to give you the long-term play, where you could ultimately go with this sales meeting process. The endgame is an evolution from you leading the sales meetings, to them conducting the sales meetings with you observing the meeting and giving them feedback.

Now that we've covered the endgame, let's get right back to the sales meeting process that we overviewed and dive into how to prepare for the meeting.

Preparation

Preparation is everything. Noah did not start building the ark when it was raining.

—Warren Buffett

Many sales managers put their meetings together at the last second, and it shows. Preparation makes for a more meaningful experience at the meeting. So, how do you prepare to conduct a sales meeting? Here are some best practices to help you get ready. Prior to the sales meeting:

- Think about what is happening with your sales team to help you formulate your agenda. For example:
  - If your team is having difficulty getting sales appointments because they are struggling with overcoming objections, you may want to have overcoming objections as the focus of your skill development training session.
  - As it relates to goal reporting/setting, you could look at your sales dashboard for metrics, win rates, average deal size, and opportunities in the pipeline to help you prepare your talking points at that point in the meeting.
- Prepare the opening inspiration, your success story, the skill development training topic you will cover, talking points for goal reporting and goal setting on how the overall team is doing against their goals, the logistics for the next meeting, and the closing inspiration.
- Select and ask a salesperson to take notes in the meeting, write the summary after the meeting, and distribute the meeting summary to all participants.
- Distribute the agenda for the sales meeting in an email or as an attachment to the calendar/Outlook meeting invitation prior to the meeting. Have it in a printed format or onscreen at the sales meeting so everyone attending can see it.
- Prepare whatever will be needed to facilitate the skill development training session. Send any materials to your salespeople prior to the meeting with instructions for how to prepare prior to coming to the meeting.
- Send an email to your salespeople and remind them to prepare for the meeting by:

- o Being ready to share a success story.
- o Reviewing and completing any pre-meeting assignment for skill development training.
- o Being ready for goal reporting/setting.
- Be prepared at game time. You are leading the meeting. Arrive at the meeting early enough to get the room set up, distribute materials, confirm technology is in place for sharing visuals, and connect with remote team members.

Welcome/Overview Agenda

Now that you're prepared for your meeting, let's overview how you will begin. You will begin by welcoming your sales team to the meeting, complimenting them for being on time, and warming up the room with relevant small talk (last night's game, the weather, current events) to create a buzz in the room. You will then briefly walk your team through the agenda for the meeting. Keep in mind that you have already sent them the agenda and it is visible to everyone in the meeting. Remote attendees should have the agenda in front of them as well. When you are prepared for the meeting and you know what you want to achieve, you come into the meeting on a mission, with a sense of purpose and confidence, knowing what you want to accomplish in that meeting. That mindset will manifest itself in your presence as you stand in front of the room and begin to overview what's going to happen in the meeting. Standing up creates more energy in the room, as opposed to sitting down. Remember, "motion creates emotion." Since you prepared before the meeting, as you overview the agenda, enthusiasm and conviction will come through in your voice, based on your personality and style as a sales manager. Your level of enthusiasm, or lack thereof, will be contagious. That could potentially set the tone for the rest of the meeting.

As you read the following example of welcoming and overviewing the agenda, read it either out loud or to yourself with a level of enthusiasm as if you were using those words to start your next sales meeting. It doesn't mean you will use them but, hopefully, you will understand conceptually that, when you start a sales meeting, you need to sweep them into what is going to happen in the meeting with enthusiasm.

Sales manager: Welcome everybody and thanks for being on time. You're awesome. Let me give you a quick overview of what we're going to do in the meeting today. First, we're going to start with an opening inspiration to get the meeting off on a positive note. After that, one at a time, everybody will get on their feet and share a success story with the rest of the team. Then we're going to focus on skill development training. Our topic for today is how to handle the objection, "I'm happy with my current supplier." Next, we are going to move on to goal reporting and goal setting, where everybody on the team will report what they set out to do and what they actually did. We will then summarize any action steps that we set in the meeting and discuss the next meeting's logistics. Finally, we will end the meeting on a high note with a closing inspiration. Are you ready to go? Let's do this. Whoooo!!!

Now that you have just read this example, hopefully, you can't wait to start your next sales meeting by doing something very similar. In the laboratory of human experience over the past 35 years in coaching sales managers how to conduct productive sales meetings, we have found that there is something to be said for learning from best practices. There is also something to be said for learning from what not to do.

Don't:

- Start the meeting late.
- Start the meeting sitting down if you can stand up.
- Start the meeting by reading the agenda out loud with no eye contact with the sales team.
- Apologize for having the sales meeting.
- Start the meeting in a negative way, beginning with bad news or how sales are off.

We're sure that you have never started a sales meeting by doing any of these things that don't work. Once you have delivered the agenda with enthusiasm and your sales team is energized, you will move on to the next topic on the agenda – the opening inspiration. Keep in mind that the meeting started at 8:00 a.m. and it's now 8:02 a.m. and you're rolling.

Once you're very comfortable opening up the sales meeting the right way, and your team has bought into the sales meeting process, you may be ready to select one salesperson on your team to open the meeting with the welcome and overview of the agenda. To prepare your salesperson for this activity, refer back to Chapter 8. You will be the practice coach and use the six steps of explain, you demonstrate, practice, observe, give feedback, and they demonstrate before the meeting starts. When the meeting begins, you will observe them welcoming everyone to the meeting and overviewing the agenda. While that is happening, you will take notes. When the meeting is over, you will set aside time to deliver performance feedback and, if necessary, be the practice coach again.

Opening Inspiration

So, you've opened the meeting by welcoming everyone and overviewing the agenda. Ideally, you did it with an appropriate level of excitement and your team is feeling energized. Keep in mind that there are a number of things that could be going on in the minds of your sales team when they come to the meeting. One of the main reasons to do an opening inspiration is to redirect their thoughts from whatever they were thinking about before coming into the sales meeting and get them focused on the sales meeting in a meaningful way. It could be a story, a quote, a short video, a poem, a meme, a picture, etc. Here are some things that may be on their mind coming into the sales meeting:

I need to get a summary out for my meeting last night.

I need to prepare for my meeting today.

My emails are backing up.

I need to hit the phones today.

Wow, that drive into work sure was tough today.

Can't wait for the weekend, today is Friday.

I'm not a morning person. I need another cup of coffee.

You will begin implementing the sales meeting process by conducting the opening inspiration yourself. Over time, you will transition this activity to members of your sales team. Be the practice coach prior to the meeting. Ask your salesperson what they are going to present and have them do a few dry runs on you prior to the meeting. The opening inspiration should be brief, about 1–2 minutes. Whether you do the opening inspiration or someone on your team does the opening inspiration, if it is short like a quote, you can actually place it on the meeting agenda that will be distributed prior to the meeting. After the opening inspiration has been delivered, you can generate engagement with the team by getting them to discuss with each other how the inspiration applies to them and the job that they do every day. You can do this in several ways:

- Select certain team members to share with the team how they feel the inspiration applies to them. "[Salesperson's name], please share with the team how this opening inspiration resonates with you."
- If you chose the opening inspiration, you will go first and share what the inspiration means to you. After that, you will ask other members of the sales team what the opening inspiration means to them. "Hey team, let me share with you why I selected this opening inspiration and what I like about it. I chose it because … What I like about it is … [Salesperson's name], why don't you share with all of us what resonates with you about the opening inspiration."
- If a salesperson chose and presented the opening inspiration, have them share with the team why they selected that inspiration and how it resonates with them.
- Have each salesperson find a partner and discuss what the inspiration meant to them, then debrief with the entire group. "Hey, everybody please find a partner, take a minute, and share with each other what that opening inspiration meant to you." (Discussion takes place …) "Who would like to go first and share with us what you discussed with your partner."

Your meeting started at 8:00 a.m. and now it's 8:07 a.m. and everybody has already been actively engaged in the meeting. Now it's time to move into success stories.

Success Stories

We are all storytellers. We all live in a network of stories. There isn't a stronger connection between people than storytelling.
—Jimmy Neil Smith

Because sales is a profession that can have disappointments and failures, it is important to keep your team focused on achievements and success. One way to do this is to share success stories at your sales meetings. These stories:

- Give your salespeople ideas from their peers on what's working.
- Motivate your sales team to start doing the activities they know they should be doing but are not doing.
- Reinforce activities they are doing that are producing success and inspire them to keep doing them.
- Remind them of activities they used to do but stopped doing and motivate them to start doing those activities again.
- Create an environment where your team is sharing best practices with each other.

One reason success stories work so well is that most people love to hear an interesting story. A well-told story has the ability to grab our attention, captivate us, and create a deeper connection. When it is done right, it can be a very powerful tool. Stories paint a picture.

Sales Manager Leads with a Success Story

You will begin the success story part of the meeting, leading by example and sharing the first success story. You will set the tone and demonstrate what a success story can sound like. An easy way to transition into your success story is by saying: "The success story I would like to share with you since our last meeting is ... " Below are some example success stories.

Sales manager: The success story I would like to share with you since our last meeting is yesterday morning in our daily huddle we practiced responding to objections. I appreciated the practice and put a lot of effort into it. When I got back to my desk, I put some of the talking points we practiced in front of me to get myself ready to handle any objections that might come up on my calls. What I found was that, true to form, some of the same objections that we typically get came up. Because of my preparation, I used those talking points to handle the objections and I closed three out of my first five calls. Based on this experience, my advice to you is practice handling objections before you start taking calls.

Sales manager: The success story I would like to share with you since our last meeting is about last week when I was making calls to prospects in my target market. As I was interacting with them, I felt that my value proposition was going on a bit too long. By the time I got done with it, they were coming back immediately by saying "I'm not interested." Or "I'm already working with somebody else." So, I decided after one of my morning call blitzes to change my strategy. I basically cut my value proposition in half and, right after I presented my value proposition, I immediately asked a question. What I found was that this enabled me to get the prospect talking and engaged in the conversation and I was able to set more meetings. Based on this experience, my advice to you is the sooner you ask questions on a call, the better the call will go.

Sales manager: The success story I would like to share with you since our last meeting is, I always find my energy drops a little toward the end of my shift. My voice is not as enthusiastic at 3:00 in the afternoon as it is at 8:00 in the morning. So, the first thing I started to do was stand up for my calls in the afternoon. I found myself beginning to move around and my energy actually increased. I noticed my voice tone was as fresh on my later calls as it was at the beginning of the day. Based on this experience, my advice to you is get on your feet and move around while you're taking calls if your energy drops at the end of the day.

We've established that you are kicking off this part of the meeting with your own success story and you have a structure for beginning and ending your story. Why not start doing it in your next sales meeting? The time is now.

How to Conduct the Success Stories Segment of Your Sales Meetings

When it comes time to conduct success stories in your sales meetings, you will always go first unless you have coached and trained one of your salespeople to kick off the success stories themselves. Sharing success stories is one element of a sales meeting that will probably never change. When you send the agenda before the meeting, they will know they need to be ready to present their success story. If you are in a crunch for time and you are only able to get one segment of your meeting done, the topic you will choose is the topic your salespeople like the most, which are success stories.

To get success stories going in your sales meetings, the very first time you introduce the topic on the agenda, you may want to combine the 15-minute success story segment of the meeting with the 15-minute skill development session on how to tell a success story. You will do the skill development training (on how to tell a success story) first, then each salesperson will share their success story. So, the sequence on the agenda will be reversed this one time only. The way you set up the skill development training may sound something like this:

Sales manager: What we're going to work on today is how to share success stories in our sales meetings. Why this is important is that sharing these stories with each other will give you ideas and best practices that you can use immediately. How we're going to do it is simple. First, I will explain to you the framework of how to tell a success story. Then, I will demonstrate what it might sound like. Then, we will practice. How the practice will work is that everybody in the room will stand up and find a partner to practice their success story with. You will each get 1 minute to practice your story with your partner. To keep you on time, when you hear me say the word "ten," you'll know you have 10 seconds left to complete your story. At that point in time, regardless of where you are in your story, you should begin to transition into "based on this experience, my advice to you is ... " so that you can finish your story within a minute. (Sales manager demonstrates a success story ...) Everybody, please stand up and find a partner. One person, raise your hand, look at your partner and say, "I'll go first." Person number one, you have 60 seconds to practice your success story with your partner. Please begin ... Ten. Now, person number two, you have 60 seconds to practice your success story with your partner. Please begin ... Ten. (Repeat the practice three more times with three different partners ...)

> *If you have an apple and I have an apple and we exchange these apples then you and I will still each have one apple. But if you have an idea and I have an idea and we exchange these ideas, then each of us will have two ideas.*
> —George Bernard Shaw

Tips for Conducting the Success Stories Segment of Your Sales Meetings

- Have each salesperson stand up when presenting their success story, if they are attending in person.
- You will be the biggest advocate in the meeting by leading with applause after each success story is shared.
- Your role is to call on each salesperson, one at a time, one right after the other, so each person can share their story. Pace is important. You will know when you are doing this well if there is a hum in the room throughout the entire segment of sharing success stories.
- Limit your comments between stories to just a few words. For example, "Nice job with your time blocking. [Next salesperson's name], please go next." "Great work with the executive summary. [Next salesperson's name], please go next." "Way to track your activity last month. [Next salesperson's name], please go next." It should basically be story, brief comment with applause, story, brief comment with applause, story, brief comment with applause.
- Limit each success story to 1 minute. Over time, as your sales team becomes more proficient with their public-speaking skills, their stories may end up becoming longer. They enjoy being in front of the team and want more stage time. You need to limit this, or you will move off the timing on your agenda.

- Keep time. Let them know they have a minute to communicate their story. When there are 10 seconds left to go, say "ten."
- To encourage your team to communicate the lesson of the story, coach them to conclude their success story with "Based on this experience, my advice to you is ... "
- When you conduct skill development training on how to deliver a success story, give them examples of what lessons learned might sound like. This will be very beneficial. When doing this, try to keep it short, sweet, and actionable. For example:

   Based on this experience, my advice to you is ...
   - Plan your work and work your plan.
   - Get in to work on time.
   - Vary your voicemail messages.
   - Set daily prospecting goals.
   - Don't let negative people affect your attitude.
   - Ask for the order.
   - Follow the call flow.
   - Practice conducting the meeting before you go into the meeting.
   - Prepare your objection responses before you make outbound calls.

      These success stories will help your team members to ...
   - Become more confident speaking in public.
   - Further develop their ability to be concise.
   - Better sell themselves and their ideas.
   - Tell a compelling story anywhere.
   - Improve their leadership skills.

At this point, everybody has had a public-speaking experience sharing successes, received recognition for their success both from you and their peers, and there is a lot of positive energy in the room. Over time, if conducted well, sharing success stories will probably be your salespeople's favorite part of the sales meeting.

Skills Development Training

Nice work. You have had an opening inspiration, and everyone has shared a success story. Your meeting started at 8:00 a.m. and now it's 8:22 a.m. and you already have two wins under your belt. Your sales meeting is already better than 99% of any other sales meeting that has been conducted so far this week. There has been inspiration, ideas, best practices, and successes shared, all within 17 minutes. Now it is time to transition into the next segment on the agenda, which is skill development training.

One ready-made opportunity to help your company maximize their investment in sales training is to reinforce and revisit elements of the training in bite-size pieces in your sales meeting. Adult learners learn best when they have been given a large body of information to learn, and then revisit it in smaller chunks over time. In doing so, the likelihood of them adopting, adapting, and implementing what they have learned increases. Because the sales meeting is regularly scheduled on the calendar, it is an opportunity to reinforce your company's sales process and methodology.

Think about what most likely has taken place in your company. There was probably some type of a roll-out of your sales process and methodology in the organization. Many of the senior leaders in the sales organization were probably thinking that a miracle would happen – every salesperson in the organization would have 100% buy-in, leave the training and execute the sales process and methodology flawlessly. It's almost like they think it is a software installation: load it and it runs. But what we have discovered in working with our clients is that this is typically not the case.

What we have observed that does work is implementing a sustainment plan that reinforces and revisits the sales training relentlessly. One of the best settings to do this in is a sales meeting, because most companies have consistent meetings. The driving force of this sustainment plan in the meeting is you. Either you are going to reinforce it in the sales meeting, or you're not.

> *Practice every time you get a chance.*
>
> —Bill Monroe

Why Sales Managers Fail at Skill Development Training

From the years we have been in this business, here are some things we have observed for why an organization's sales process and methodology are not being revisited or reinforced in sales meetings. The number one observation we have made is, "It's the sales manager."

Let's overview some of the reasons why sales managers fail to, or fail at, conducting skill development training in sales meetings. Some of these reasons are of their own making, and some aren't:

- They don't know how.
- They don't think it will add value.
- They are afraid their sales team will resist.
- They mistakenly assume that their experienced salespeople are effective.
- They are actually not conducting a sales meeting. It is an operations meeting, status update, gripe session, and the sales manager talks the whole time.
- As with a workout at the gym, it's easy to procrastinate because it is not screaming, "I'm urgent and I'm important!"
- As a segment, it tends to get moved off the meeting agenda because it takes time, is difficult to do, and, when done effectively, makes everybody uncomfortable.
- There is a perception that many of the members of their sales team don't like to "role-play." Here is a tip for you – never say "role-play." Always say "practice." It's undeniable that people get better with practice. They can't NOT get better.

Forget About Role-Playing

Many salespeople have had a bad experience with "role-playing" in the past that has shaped their attitude and mindset about it. From our observations, the minute you start talking about practice in a training environment, they hear "role-play." This negative association they have with "roleplay" impacts their openness to practice. "Role-play" often fails in execution because:

- It is not clear what skill or process they are supposed to be practicing, so they revert to whatever they would normally do.
- The setup is too broad, ambiguous, or tried to cover too much at one time.

- There is no accountability to earnestly and intently participate in the practice activity, so they don't do it.
- The time allotted was too long or too short, so the time was not well spent.

Let's put aside the term "role-play" for a moment and think back to the parallel between sales coaching and athletics: professional athletes are able to deliver an astonishing variety of moves without hesitation, consistently delivering what specific plays call for. Skilled salespeople are the same: they are able to demonstrate a variety of intentional behaviors without hesitation, consistently delivering what the specific situation calls for. In each case they are able to do this thanks to repetitive practice and refinement over time in real-life situations. Some people prefer terms like "practice," "dress rehearsal," or "dry run." ("Drill" is not the most popular choice, but athletes don't seem to object to it.) Use whatever term you prefer when making your introduction to the skill development training segment, to generate buy-in with your sales team.

How to Transition to Skill Development Training

Much like the example of how to transition into the opening inspiration and the success stories, here is an example for the transition into skill development training.

Sales manager: Great job everybody on those success stories. One of the things we're committed to in every one of our sales meetings as a company is to revisit and reinforce our sales process and sales methodology, one skill at a time. I sent you an email prior to the meeting outlining the agenda and the skill development topic we will be covering, which is how to use talking points to differentiate ourselves from our competitors. Is everybody ready to go?

(Sales team responds enthusiastically: Bring it on!!!)

Sales manager: What we're going to work on today is how to use features, bridges, and benefits as a technique to highlight our uniqueness, how we're different, our advantages, and how we're better, when we are in a bake-off and the prospect asks us

"Why should we work with you?"

Why this is important is that we are in a highly competitive industry and it is becoming more and more difficult to differentiate yourself from the competition. How we're going to do it is simple. First of all, we are going to revisit what features, bridges, and benefits are. I will explain them to you one more time, because sometimes being reminded of what to do is more beneficial than learning something new. Then, I will demonstrate what some of them might sound like if I were asked the question

"Why should I work with you?"

and I will respond with three features, bridges, and benefits that differentiate us from our competitors. Then, we will practice. How the practice will work is that everybody in the room will stand up and find a partner to practice three differentiating features, bridges, and benefits with. You will each get 1 minute to communicate your three with your partner. To keep you on time, when you hear me say the word "ten," you'll know you have 10 seconds left to complete your three features, bridges, and benefits. At that point in time, regardless of where you are in your presentation, you should begin to summarize what our three differentiators are.

(Sales manager demonstrates three features, bridges, and benefits)

Sales manager: Everybody, please stand up and find a partner. One person, raise your hand, look at your partner and say,

"I'll go first."

Person number one, you have 60 seconds to practice your three differentiators with your partner. Please begin ...

(Salesperson number one practices)

Sales manager: Ten. Now, person number two, you have 60 seconds to practice your three differentiators with your partner. Please begin ...

(Salesperson number two practices)

Sales manager: Ten.

(Repeat the practice two more times with two different partners ...)

Sales manager: Thanks for doing that. Everybody, please take your seat. Now we're going to go around the table clockwise, one at a time, and each of you will have an opportunity to stand up and communicate to us your three differentiators. You each have 1 minute. [Salesperson's name], please begin.

You will then follow the same exact process you did when conducting success stories. One salesperson stands up and communicates three differentiators. You will give a few words of feedback. The next person stands up and communicates their three differentiators. You will give a few words of feedback.

Skill Development Training Tips

- Work on one skill at a time.
- Work on a manageable chunk of a skill in which the sales process is broken down into smaller pieces.
- Be very specific about how you position the skill they are about to practice – what you are going to do, why it should be important to them, and how you are going to practice.
- Be prepared to deliver a world-class demonstration of the skill.
- When your sales team is practicing with each other, observe them and give them feedback.
- When you feel they have reached an acceptable level of competency with the skill, ask them to return to their seats and have each one stand individually and give an uninterrupted demonstration in front of the sales team without any notes.

* * *

Now that you have completed skill development training, it's 8:37 a.m. and you're more than halfway through the meeting. Look at what you have accomplished. Everybody is motivated, success stories have been shared, a skill has been reinforced and refined, and every salesperson on your team has demonstrated their competency with that skill.

Skill development training may be another activity you will want to transition to a member of your sales team at some point. The major benefit of your salespeople conducting skill development training in the meeting through coaching their peers is that they will learn the skill more deeply by training others. Be the practice coach prior to the meeting. Ask your salesperson what skill they would like to reinforce in the skill development session of the meeting and have them practice it multiple times with you prior to the meeting.

Goal Reporting and Goal Setting

A sales meeting provides an excellent opportunity to track goals because, when your salespeople report their goals in front of the rest of their peers, it adds an extra element of accountability to the process. It is a healthy way to share results and increase commitment to each other. It is important that you share and report how the team is performing against the team's goals so that every salesperson knows where the team stands in relation to the overall team goals. After that, each team member will report their individual goal, what they set out to do, and what they actually did.

There are multiple ways to conduct the goal reporting/goal setting portion of the meeting. Here are a few ideas:

- Have a scoreboard pre-populated with each salesperson's numbers, goals versus actual. Have each salesperson explain their numbers and provide feedback on what worked or didn't work.
- Have your scoreboard color-coded based on your team's results for specific key performance indicators (KPIs) that you want to focus attention on in the meeting. One important KPI that many sales managers focus on is new quality opportunities that go into the top end of the sales team's pipeline. The reason they put emphasis on this is because what goes into the top of the pipeline typically drives what comes out the bottom of the pipeline. For example, let's say you wanted to highlight the importance of identifying new opportunities with your sales team as the one KPI you wanted to emphasize in the goal reporting/setting of the meeting. Here is an example way to color-code results based on the KPI:
  o Green: exceeded new opportunity identification goal.
  o Yellow: met new opportunity identification goal.
  o Red: did not meet new opportunity identification goal.
  o Blue: personal best of new opportunity identification goal.

- Have a blank scoreboard ready and have each salesperson on your team walk up to the board and post their goals vs. actual, either before the meeting starts or during the meeting. This creates not only the accountability of them knowing their numbers, but also the positive peer pressure that manifests itself when they walk up in front of their peers and write their numbers on the scoreboard.
- Regardless of how you decide to do goal reporting and goal setting in your sales meetings, you can ask your salespeople questions when you are reviewing the numbers, such as:

  What went well?

  What led to your success? (when they exceed their goal)

  What obstacles did you face?

  What challenges did you run up against? (when they miss a goal)

Keep the Reporting Short and Sweet

Having participated in hundreds of sales meetings with our clients, we have learned that, when you are in the goal reporting/goal setting segment of the meeting and your sales team is reporting their numbers, only ask one question after they have reported their numbers. We have found that, when additional questions are asked, the lengthy conversation tends to cause the meeting to drag on and run over the allotted time. Let's get into a real-life scenario. Here's the setting: you are the sales manager and are leading a meeting with the 10 salespeople on your team in a conference room, and you have 15 minutes allocated on the agenda for goal reporting and goal setting. You are running on time right now and don't want to run over. Here is an example of what this segment of the meeting might sound like.

Sales manager: Great job everybody. Well done with demonstrating three different capabilities we have that separate us from our competitors. I congratulate all of you for doing it on your feet in front of everybody, because each one of you put your own spin on why we're unique. I think that really gave everybody else on the team additional ideas on how they can better communicate our differentiators in the marketplace.

So, let's move to the next item on the agenda, which is goal reporting and goal setting. I'm going to kick it off by giving you a status update with where we stand mid-year, in terms of the progress we've made towards achieving our goal for the year. After that, each one of you, one at a time, will have the opportunity to stand up and share with the team the goal(s) you set in our last meeting and what you actually did. We will not have enough time to dig into all of the details of what everybody on the team did since we last met. Realistically, we will have time to ask two or three of you to share with us what you did well, what worked, how you achieved your personal best last month, and what advice you would give your peers. If you fell short of a KPI, we might generate some group-think right here in the meeting by asking you what obstacles you encountered in attempting to achieve your goals, because we are certain that your peers may have some ideas that could help you.

(Sales manager displays the pre-populated scoreboard, then overviews where the team is in terms of goal achievement year to date)

> *Take a minute; look at your goals, look at your performance, see if your behavior matches your goals.*
>
> —Ken Blanchard

Goal-Reporting and Goal-Setting Tips

- Sales manager goes first.
- Have everybody stand up while they are reporting their numbers.
- You transition from one salesperson to the next with minimal comment to maintain the flow and the timing. One of the fundamental elements that make goal reporting and goal setting work is that once they have said the numbers, they've said it all. Performance is reality. It is very common after everybody states their numbers for nobody to say anything. Oftentimes, when the numbers are great, comments from the salesperson's teammates are complimentary and when the numbers come up short, the comments from the team are typically supportive.

- You can rotate the key performance indicators that you want to focus attention on in goal reporting and goal setting from meeting to meeting.
- If you highlight three people in one meeting for success against the goals, you may want to highlight different salespeople in the next meeting.

* * *

Now that you have completed goal reporting and goal setting, it's 8:52 a.m. and you're almost done. Look at what you have accomplished. Everybody has been motivated, success stories have been shared, a skill has been reinforced and refined, every salesperson on your team has demonstrated their competency with that skill, you have completed goal reporting and goal setting, and given praise and recognition for performance.

Goal reporting and goal setting may be another activity you will want to transition to a member of your sales team over time. The major benefit of your salespeople conducting goal reporting and goal setting in the meeting is that it creates a great sense of accountability. Be the practice coach prior to the meeting. Ask your salesperson what KPI they would like to focus on and have them practice goal reporting/goal setting multiple times with you prior to the meeting.

Summary and Action Steps

Prior to the meeting, you will have selected one of your salespeople to take notes during the meeting and document any action steps that come out of the meeting. You will have them briefly review the notes they took and the action items agreed upon by the team. When the meeting is over, they will take the notes and email the sales team a summary of what happened in the meeting and any action steps to be taken. It is very important that everyone is clear on what is expected from them after the meeting. It also allows for no misinterpretation on what happened during the meeting and what is to happen next. You have just summarized action steps and it's not 8:55.

Next-Meeting Logistics

At this point, you will communicate the date and time for the next meeting. If you are at the point where members of your sales team are running segments of the meeting, you may want to announce or select who will lead parts of the next meeting. Now it's 8:57 a.m. and you're about to begin the closing inspiration.

Closing Inspiration

End the meeting with a bang. Just like the way you started it. Your salespeople should leave the meeting positive, motivated, and ready to make things happen. Now it's 9:00 a.m. and you had a great meeting. Go get 'em tiger! ROAR!!!

Other Activities

Here is a list of some other topics that you could put on an agenda to add variety and value to your sales meetings.

- **Case studies:** Have a few members of your sales team come prepared to share the details of recent opportunities they have closed. How they got the meeting, how they closed the deal, and any issues, objections, challenges, or concerns they addressed in the process.
- **Guest speakers:** Bring in other key people from different departments in the company. For example, an operations director, customer service manager, chief financial officer, etc. You can also have someone come in from outside the company such as a product representative from one of your vendors.
- **Senior management guest:** Invite an area, regional, or divisional manager who may be in town to give an update of what's happening in the company.
- **Book of the month club:** Read a sales book as a team and discuss it at the meeting. You could assign different chapters of the book to different salespeople on the team as homework to lead a discussion in the next meeting.

- **Deal diagnosis:** Your salespeople share with each other opportunities that are stuck, stalled, not moving forward to the next step. Brainstorm ideas on what they can do to get the prospect to move forward.
- **Pipeline updates:** Have every salesperson on the team give a quick status check on their pipeline. This can be a little bit different from goal setting and goal reporting but it's another form of accountability.
- **Competitive analysis:** This is an opportunity for your sales team to share anything they've learned about the competition. Their strengths, their weaknesses, and especially why prospects decided to work with them as opposed to you.
- **Subject matter expert speaker:** Subject matter experts are a good source of product and industry knowledge. They can come from inside your company or outside your company. Ask them to share insights on their journey in the business and the industry as a whole, what their day-to-day work involves, their thoughts on the future of your industry, etc. It is very common to have multiple subject matter experts come in to speak as a panel.
- **Bring your best idea:** Have everybody come prepared to share a great sales idea such as an objection response, a discovery question, or a prospecting tip.

Most successful sales managers run great meetings. Their meetings are well thought out, planned, facilitated in an efficient manner, interactive, and positive, with successes shared and recognition given. They are perceived by the sales team as time well spent and the sales team leaves the meetings inspired and motivated. What we have attempted to provide you with in this chapter is a sales meeting framework that you can use to conduct sales meetings and, over time, delegate responsibility for conducting segments of the meeting to members of your team. There is also a list of other activities that you can use to add diversity of activity into your meetings. Think of this chapter as a sales meeting playbook. You can take this book tomorrow and open this chapter and use it as a roadmap to conduct your next sales meeting.

Takeaway Questions

Below are questions you can use for further reflection.

Takeaway Discussion Questions for Your Organization

- If you are leading a sales organization, how effective do you think your sales managers are at conducting sales meetings?
- Do you believe that they are using sales meetings as an opportunity to maximize your company's investment in sales training?
- What is the opportunity for improvement?

Takeaway Questions for Personal Reflection

- If you are leading a sales team, how effective are you at conducting sales meetings?
- Are you using them to maximize your company's investment in sales training?
- What is your opportunity for improvement?

10

Sales Huddles

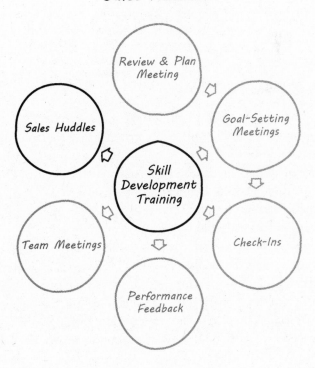

Sales Huddles

- Review & Plan Meeting
- Goal-Setting Meetings
- Sales Huddles
- Skill Development Training
- Check-Ins
- Team Meetings
- Performance Feedback

TEAMS FROM ALL DISCIPLINES rely on huddles: medicine, manufacturing, athletics, software development, financial services, and the military, to name just a few. In sales management, as in other fields, the purpose of sales huddles is to get everyone on the same page, at the same time, and send them into the game with focus and enthusiasm. Huddles typically include brief updates, recognition, skills reinforcement, accountability, and motivation.

Sales huddles are essentially condensed versions of sales meetings that are shorter in duration and held more frequently. Generally speaking, the frequency of sales meetings and huddles is directly related to the length of the typical sales cycle. For example, a team of financial advisors building their pipeline might have a team sales meeting once a week and a huddle once a day. Most contact center teams have huddles every day at the start of the shift. Find the right frequency for your team. Sales huddles should be quick and inspiring, and highlight a sales skill. Don't let operational issues overwhelm the agenda. Keep a "parking lot" for problem solving and other items better addressed at a later time.

> *I want to go to practice. I want to be in the huddles. That's me.*
> —University of Tennessee women's basketball coach
> Pat Summit

Benefits of Sales Huddles

For some reason, a lot of companies have an overinflated view of their salespeople and seem reluctant to disturb the goose that lays the golden eggs. In our experience, though, successful salespeople appreciate having a thoughtful and disciplined approach to the day, week, month, and year, just like successful athletes or performing artists. (In fact, they would expect nothing less, and if it didn't come from their sales manager, they would do it themselves.)

Starting the week off with a sales huddle at 7:00 or 8:00 a.m. Monday morning is a good example. It ensures 100% of your team is ready to get to work. Think about it: certain military and medical teams would never start a day, or an operation, without a briefing. Sales may not be a matter of life or death, but it's important enough that you need to have your act together, right? So, let's walk through some of the benefits of sales huddles.

Recognition

At a recent conference hosted by the Association of Talent Development, Dan Ariely wondered aloud about why people are so cheap with compliments, when they actually cost nothing. Why do we use the word "pay" a compliment when it is free? Maybe because to the person on the receiving end it is the most valued currency of all.

> When we are acknowledged for our work, we are willing to work harder for less pay, and when we are not acknowledged, we lose much of our motivation. (Ariely 2016, 281)

Positive recognition is one of the most profound motivators for human beings. People want to be seen and acknowledged. Recognition makes salespeople feel good about themselves and motivates them to continue doing the things that attracted attention. Meanwhile, other members of the sales team are probably aspiring – consciously or unconsciously—to enjoy similar recognition in the future.

Accountability

In a sales huddle, salespeople will be reporting on their activities and results, compared to their previous commitments. If they overachieve their goals, recognition is given. If they don't achieve their goals, there is a sort of public reckoning. Salespeople fall short of their goal for a variety of reasons. They may have missed work due to illness or some other issue. They may have lacked the tools or resources needed to complete the activities they planned and committed to. In these examples, the situation was outside their control, there's no harm, no foul. But if the weather was good, everyone was healthy, the Wi-Fi was up, the mobile signal was good, they had the tools, they had the knowledge, and they had the resources (basically, success was 100% in their control), and they still fell short, then there is going to be a "What's up?" moment.

Sales huddles should be all about team support and solidarity. You are committed to the success of the whole team. If a salesperson on the team is not confident in their skills, you will coach them. If their motivation is lagging, which happens to everyone now and then, you can revisit the connection between their activities and their personal goals. If it becomes clear over time that the role is not a good fit for a particular individual, it is better to know that sooner, with more data, as compared to later, without it.

Success Stories

If every huddle included sales success stories, think how many ideas will be shared throughout the course of a year. Each story may only be a minute long, but they add up to a boatload of collective experience. Sharing ideas reinforces the behavior in the mind of the person telling the story. In other words, they are more likely to repeat the behavior in the future because they endorsed it publicly (Cialdini 2007). Being asked to share successes is also a form of recognition. Even though the opportunity may rotate to everyone on the team, every individual still feels special when sharing their secrets of success. Sharing successes is also a form of social proof, or consensus. The psychology is, if my peers are doing it, maybe it will work for me too.

Skill Development Training

As you well know by now, we recommend skill development training in most sales coaching activities, and the huddle is no exception. The key to executing skills training in a 15-minute meeting is to be an expert with the facilitation of the practice activities. Over time, the responsibility for facilitating skill activities should be delegated to top performers at first, and eventually, extended to the entire team. One of the side benefits of learning how to coach is becoming more open to being coached oneself. When everyone on the team is both a coach and a learner, depending on the day, everyone can lighten up, resist the temptation to take themselves too seriously, focus on improving their performance, and have some fun along the way.

Relevant Updates

Huddles are a good time to give updates if they are limited to things that are very timely and have an immediate impact on the sales activity of the day. Anything else can wait for a team sales meeting. This guideline is not an absolute, but more of an insurance policy to make sure that (brief) huddles stay purely focused on sales performance.

Building Bench Strength

As noted above, huddles provide a great opportunity for emerging leaders to develop their ability to conduct skill development training and share best practices with other salespeople on the team. If you are conducting your sales huddles consistently as recommended, there will be numerous opportunities for development. Plus, it takes the burden off you to do the sales huddle all the time.

Inspiration

Rejection is a way of life for salespeople. It helps if they pick themselves up, take a deep breath, and consider things from a broader perspective. When a salesperson selects and delivers an opening or closing inspiration, it reveals something about the person who chose it. The other salespeople on the team will typically respond with empathy to this vulnerability and, therefore, unite.

How to Recognize Effective Sales Huddles

Effective huddles share certain characteristics. Much like in Chapter 9, there are certain elements of a sales huddle that are essential. Here are a few.

They Happen at a Consistent Time and Place

Conducting your sales huddles consistently at the same time every day is the most fundamental best practice of effective huddles because that routine sets the expectation that everyone will be there, on time, every time. It is also efficient because it eliminates the need to schedule each individual meeting. If you lead a virtual team, conducting sales huddles consistently at the same time every day can be even more important, because it may be the only opportunity you will have during the day to check in with your entire team, together, in real time.

They are Brief (10–15 Minutes) and Focused

Selling time is precious and anything that takes away from that time had better add value. Sales huddles can be brief, yet highly effective, if they follow the same agenda every time. A well-organized and -executed sales huddle shows your team that you value their time and are prepared to deliver value back to them. A sales huddle should be brief enough, and motivational enough, to get your sales team off to a great start for the day.

They Start on Time and End on Time

How do you feel when meetings start late? Like you could be doing other things? How do you feel when they run over? Like you want to move on to other things? Your sales team is no different. Starting and ending on time demonstrates respect and professionalism.

They Have 100% Mandatory Participation

Under normal circumstances, we expect 100% attendance at huddles and no phones unless required by the agenda (e.g. reading an opening or closing inspiration). Each team member rotates responsibility for the various parts of the agenda, as directed by you. This relieves you of having to do everything, and it gives your salespeople a chance to enhance their skills and confidence in front of their peers.

They Don't Get Derailed

Effective sales huddles avoid getting derailed by operational issues or problem solving. You can put these items in the "parking lot." Make sure to follow up on the items after the meeting so your team has confidence that, when they surface issues in the huddle, you will loop back with them.

They May Be Called Spontaneously

A pre-shift huddle in a contact center is like a pre-game huddle, it's done at the same time every day. You can also take time out during the day and call a quick huddle when needed. In the course of the day something may happen that you want to bring to the attention of the team. It could be something new that you know your salespeople may need to react to in real time. Or, it could be spontaneous recognition for a job well done.

They Assume Everyone Wants to Improve

When you implement the principles in this book, you'll build a culture in which everyone expects to focus on improving some aspect of their performance every day. It could be reactive to an identified skill gap. Or it could be proactive. It could be directed by the sales manager, or it could be requested by the salesperson.

For example, in working with one of our clients, the sales process included about a dozen key skill areas. For each skill, a color-coded "tick sheet" was developed that included best practices, example scripting, and blank boxes for tracking on-call behaviors. At the start of each shift, each salesperson would select a skill they wanted to work on and

15-Minute Sales Huddle Agenda

Huddle Agenda	(Floor)	Monday, Jan 27 7:00-7:15 a.m.
Topic	Minutes Allotted	Cumulative Time
Opening Inspiration	2	7:02
Success Stories	2	7:04
KPI Reporting	2	7:06
Skill Development Training	5	7:11
Focus of the Day	2	7:13
Closing Inspiration	2	7:15

Figure 10.1   Sales Huddle Agenda

take the appropriate color-coded tick sheet back to their workstation. Throughout the day, the sales managers would walk the floor. They could tell from the color of the tick sheet what each salesperson was working on for that day, which enabled them to give positive feedback throughout the day in recognition of the focused effort being made by the team to build optimal habits.

Sales Huddle Example Scripting

What we're going to introduce you to is some example scripting to help you prepare for your next sales huddle. These are just some example talking points you can refer to as ideas to build your own. You can also use this as a resource to coach members of your sales team to conduct different elements of a huddle.

Opening Inspiration – Salesperson on the Team Opens the Meeting with the Inspiration

Salesperson: Good morning everyone! For today I chose a quote from the author and poet Maya Angelou, who said "People won't remember what you said, but they will remember how you made them feel." I chose that because it helps me take focus off of myself and put myself into the shoes of the customers.

Success Story – Salesperson on the Team Shares Their Success Story

Salesperson: When calling on the prospects in my territory, I got into a bad habit of opening the conversation with how great we are without taking an interest in them. Last week I switched it around and opened every conversation by asking them questions about their situation, and then looked for ways to link to our products. It was amazing how much more interested people were in talking. Based on this experience, my advice to you is, open every conversation by making it about them, not you.

Reporting – Sales Manager Leads Reporting

Sales manager: I'd like to go around, starting with [Salesperson's name], reporting on your calls, emails, social network connections, and leads for yesterday.

For successes: *Way to go! Keep it going!*

For gaps/shortfalls: *What will you keep, start, or stop doing?*

Skill Development Training – Sales Manager Conducts Skill Development Training

Sales manager: Team, what we're going to work on today is how to communicate the features and benefits of our new product line. Why this is important to you is because it is a brand new line, our customers want to hear about it, and the more confident and capable we are, the better we can get this new product off the ground. Here is how we're going to do it: I will explain how to communicate the features and benefits of the new product line. Then, I will demonstrate what it might sound like. Then we will practice. Everybody will work with a partner and you will each go back and forth until you feel confident in your ability to use the features, bridges, and benefits of the new product line in conversations with our customers. I'll observe you and give you feedback as you practice to help you get better faster. When we're done, one of you will have the opportunity to demonstrate to the team that you got it. How does that sound?

Focus of the Day/Goals – Sales Manager Leads Focus of the Day

Sales manager: Everyone has a tick sheet with something you are going to focus on for today, right? I will be stopping by a little bit later this morning to check your progress. Remember to keep call notes on your focus area so we can talk about it later.

Closing Inspiration – Salesperson Leads the Closing Inspiration

Salesperson: For the closing inspiration today, I chose a quote from football player Jerry Rice, who said "Today I'll do what others won't.

Tomorrow I'll do what others can't." I love that quote because it reminds me it is within my power to be the best.

Sales huddles are simply a quicker, and often more regular, version of a sales meeting. Many of our clients who run a call center sales environment have a great deal of success with short, daily huddles to share success, new information, and motivate the team. In a geographically disbursed outside sales team, a daily huddle can happen over a conference call. Believe it or not, it might even be easier to prepare for a sales meeting than for a sales huddle because, if you only have 10–15 minutes to work with, you need to be able to distill all of the things you want to get done in the huddle in a very short period of time. Because huddles are so frequent, it is one of the sales coaching activities we are covering in this book that will be very easy for you to train and coach your sales team to conduct.

Takeaway Questions

Below are questions you can use for further reflection.

Takeaway Discussion Questions for Your Organization

- If you are leading a sales organization, how effective do you think your sales managers are in conducting sales huddles?
- What is their opportunity for improvement?

Takeaway Questions for Personal Reflection

- If you are leading a sales team, how effective are you at conducting sales huddles with your team?
- What is your opportunity for improvement?

11

Sales and Service Coaching in the Contact Center

WORKING IN CONTACT centers around the world for many years, we've seen some great coaches, some terrible coaches, and a lot of average coaches. What separates the best from the rest? In our experience, top coaches: prioritize time for coaching activities, effectively set expectations, consistently use non-scored feedback in addition to scored feedback, coach proactively and not just reactively, focus on one behavior or skill at a time, use questions to coach, and consistently recognize people for their accomplishments.

A Tale of Two Coaches

Meet two coaches, Bradley and Sarah. Both have 12 agents on their team, and they are required to provide 2 hours of call feedback and coaching per agent, per month.

Bradley meets with his agents for 1 hour, every 2 weeks. Typically, they listen to two or three calls that are 7–10 minutes long. For each call Bradley provides a "feedback hoagie": a couple of compliments sandwiching a pile of weaknesses and improvements he wants to see. Agents typically walk out with 6–12 items on their to-do list.

Two weeks later they meet again, listen to calls, and Bradley wonders why they have not implemented their to-do lists. Their performance metrics are flat. He gets frustrated – why won't these agents give him what he is asking for?

Sarah handles her coaching differently. She spends 30 minutes per week with each agent. Two of those sessions include a scored call. The other two are non-scored coaching sessions. In these meetings, Sarah sometimes listens to a call, or part of a call; but she always gives a long list of things the agent has done well on the call (10–12 positives). Next, they discuss and practice a sales skill and build a micro action plan to track that behavior on the next batch of calls. This takes about 20–25 minutes.

After the agent completes the activity (e.g. later in the shift or the next day), Sarah visits with the agent for 5 minutes to hear about their experience with customers and what they learned while applying the behavior. Other times, Sarah follows the same process but without listening to a call. And finally, sometimes Sarah puts the whole team on the same micro action plan at once. She uses the extra time working on other priorities.

The morale on Sarah's team is high. The agents feel valued and enjoy the challenge of trying new things to improve the customer experience. Their performance metrics are improving, and Sarah feels grateful to have such a great team.

Which coach would you rather be?

Now, let's consider seven key success factors for coaching sales and service calls in the contact center that will help make your life as a sales manager look more like Sarah's, and less like Bradley's.

Tale of Two Coaches

	Frequency	Minutes	Call Listening	O·F·I·'s	+'s	Skills Practice	Micro Action Plan	Debrief	Sessions/ Agent/ Month
Michael	Every 2 weeks	60	Always	6-12	2				2
Sarah	Weekly	30	Every Other	1-2	10-12	✓	✓	✓	4

*Opportunities for Improvement

Figure 11.1   Tale of Two Coaches

Make Time

In our experience, world-class sales and service managers in contact centers spend 15–30% of their time (6–12 hours per week) coaching, assuming a team of a dozen agents. This comes as a shock to many sales managers on the contact center projects we work on, because they spend so much time on administration, HR, and other non-sales activities. But think about it: what is your job, if not to improve the next call that comes into the team? You may have to wage a battle internally to reduce the time you spend on administration and increase the time for sales coaching. Or, your organization may choose to assign team leads or others to provide sales coaching while managers focus on other things. Either model can work, as long as someone is filling the coaching role consistently and effectively.

Set Expectations

We've noted elsewhere that if your team is not accustomed to consistent sales coaching or micro action plans it will probably take a little time for them to get over the hump. Be patient and have confidence that once they get used to the shift to a coaching culture they will be more enthusiastic, more confident, and more successful. If you are just starting out to implement the recommendations in this book, it's a good idea to level-set with your team what you are doing and why. Tell them your goal is not only to improve their selling, but also your coaching. Ask for their help in making the transition and helping everyone succeed together.

Use Non-Scored Feedback

Imagine if you sent your children to school every day, and all they ever did was take tests. Would you wonder when the teaching was going to start? Admittedly, tests are important for auditing and measuring, but they are not the best way of learning. Yet in many contact centers every quality assurance or coaching interaction is based on a scored call observation. Is the data useful? Yes! Is it the best or only way to improve the performance of the team? No!

The best way to improve the performance of the team is with a combination of scored and non-scored coaching and feedback. Why? Most people do not score 100% quality on every call – far from it. In fact, the reverse is true: most calls observed will have failure points. In fact, they used to use the term "fatal flaw" for certain types of quality assurance errors. The term is borrowed from the software development world but applied to humans. "You had a fatal error on that call." How does that feel? Focusing primarily on failure points can stir resentment or resistance. Psychologically, there can be a sense of failure. The same thing can happen when you pile on 10 OFIs (opportunities for improvement) at once.

Find opportunities to provide non-scored feedback and practice activities within one-on-one call coaching sessions, team meetings, and floor interactions. Use a call guide or quality attributes to see how many positives you can find on the call. Select a skill, scenario, or topic to practice. **It doesn't necessarily have to be something that was "failed" on the last call observation.** In fact, you can run a highly effective and efficient 15-minute session in which no calls are listened to. Instead, a customer scenario, topic, or call skill is discussed, practiced, and a micro action plan is put in place.

Quality Assurance vs. Sales Coaching

Anyone who has worked in contact centers knows that the relationship between quality assurance and sales operations is sometimes "interesting." In some cases, the relationship is adversarial: the quality assurance analysts are trying to find deficiencies and the sales managers are trying to defend the agent and negotiate for an elevated quality assurance score. In other cases, the quality assurance standards don't do a good job of measuring successful sales behaviors against technical things, for example, proper process, documentation, and disclosures. We have often encountered contact center outsourcers who beat their chests about their quality assurance scores when, in fact, the quality assurance standards didn't accurately measure, or help manage, productive sales behaviors. To put it more simply, a "good call" from a quality assurance standpoint may be a terrible call from a sales point of view. If your call center outsourcer is claiming a solid quality assurance score while their sales behavior/performance is poor, it is time to have a reality check.

Some organizations include sales behaviors in their quality assurance forms. In other cases, the quality assurance form measures technical compliance and there are separate tools for sales and sales coaching, for example, sales conversation guides and coaching feedback forms that tie into them. If you are in a situation where the quality assurance process does not result in effective sales coaching, then you should introduce separate sales coaching activities with supporting tools. There may also be opportunity in your organization to create better alignment between quality assurance standards and sales competencies and coaching.

Coach Proactively

It is common sense that we need to observe our salespeople selling in order to help them improve, and that is why in many contact center teams, the call coaching is 100% reactive. That is a liability. Always-scored coaching can have a negative impact on motivation, but it also takes longer (usually twice as long). How can you improve skills without call observation? The first situation is when you are aware that a rep has a skill gap and you know what the micro action plan(s) should look like. You just put them on the MAP (micro action plan) without a call observation. The second situation is like coaching an athletic team: while coaches do watch video and provide feedback on live performance, they also spend at least as much time proactively practicing plays and individual skills. They don't always need to wait for the game films to plan a practice.

Remember our "Tale of Two Coaches"? If you have 12 agents on your team and you normally observe and coach each one for 30–60 minutes per week, that is 6–12 hours per week. What would happen if you alternated individual (personalized) action plans with whole-team activities? If you gave the same micro action plan to the whole team on a MAP Tracker to be completed within the shift, the following things will happen:

- You will get 6–12 hours back into your schedule for the week.
- You can literally watch your entire team focus on improving their performance: one skill at a time, one call at a time, and one day at a time.

- You can immediately identify people who need coaching for either will, skill, or attitude.
- You will know that everyone is going to share the wealth of their experience with the rest of the team.
- You don't have to get in debates with your reps about the action plan. It wasn't assigned because they supposedly "failed" on a call. It's a team practice activity and everyone is doing the same thing.

Focus on One Behavior at a Time

Business results are a snapshot in time, and they are always yesterday's news. We can't impact the results directly, but we can impact the behaviors that generate the numbers. The performance metrics tracked in contact centers reflect things that happen in thousands and thousands of customer conversations every day. Everyone has habits, and most agents repeat certain things on many of their calls. Habitual associate behaviors impact the customer experience in those calls, including whether the customer makes a purchase, cancels a service, or escalates. The way to improve results is to get much more specific about all the behaviors that impact the quality of a customer's experience, and then to build those behaviors into habits through consistent coaching interactions.

Many managers make the mistake of addressing too many topics at once because they feel like they have to give feedback on everything they notice, especially the gaps. But this is ineffective because people simply can't change 12 habits at once.

If you think about the way people learn athletic skills (like serving a tennis ball) or musical skills (like improvising blues in the key of E on a guitar), it's a matter of demonstration, imitation/practice, repetition,

Habits to Metrics

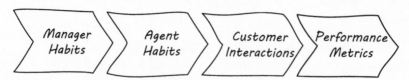

Figure 11.2   Habits to Metrics

and feedback. Verbal skills are just the same. People can change verbal habits very rapidly if you give them one thing at a time to work on for a limited duration and then debrief. Embrace it: it is your responsibility to set your agents up for success by knowing the skills, coaching the skills, writing strong micro action plans, driving accountability around those plans, and providing consistent opportunities for debrief, reflection, and forward action planning (rinse and repeat ...).

Use "MAPs" – Micro Action Plans

A MAP is a behavior-focused S.M.A.R.T. goal designed to be completed within a few hours, or perhaps a full shift. Here are the steps:

- *Identify a specific behavior.* This should be something you can observe and measure; for example, the number of discovery questions asked on the call (and about what).
- *Plan how to apply it on the job and track it.* Because we are interrupting old habits and building new ones, it is best to have some physical activity associated with the behavior, for example writing on a tick sheet, flipping coins, or placing coins in a cup. Focus intently on one behavior for a limited period of time, such as 15 calls, or 4 hours.
- *Debrief.* Talk about the activity as soon as possible after it is completed because that helps people integrate their experience and gives you a chance to recognize their effort.

Micro Action Plan

✓ Specific
  Behaviors
✓ Limited
  Window
✓ Tracking
✓ Follow Up

Figure 11.3   Micro Action Plan

MAP Tracker: 3 Discovery Questions

On my next 20 calls I will ask at least 3 discovery questions about what the customer wants and why. I will make 3 check marks in each box and write down a word representing the customer's "why".

1	2	3	4	5
6	7	8	9	10
11	12	13	14	15
16	17	18	19	20

Day: Start time: Stop time:

What went well:

Challenges:

Advice I would give to my peers:

Things I will focus on in the future:

Figure 11.4   MAP Tracker

- *Repeat.* Agree on a new micro action plan or agree to develop one during the next one-on-one call coaching session.

Best Practices for MAPs

Set clear expectations around how to complete any MAP activity, including when you will follow up. Check back through the day to create urgency and accountability. Use a MAP Tracker like the one pictured to make sure team members are making some kind of (very brief) notation on each call. This helps the learning process, proves they did the activity, creates a sense of accomplishment, and gives them focused experience they can discuss with their manager and peers. We like to use questions like these for debriefing the activity, whether one-on-one or in a team setting:

What went well?

What were the challenges?

What advice would you give to your peers regarding learning this skill and selling with this skill?

What are some things you will focus on in the future to build on what you have learned and continue to improve your performance?

It is an important part of learning to reflect on experience. When the debrief occurs in a team meeting, it provides the opportunity for social learning, collaboration, and team alignment on the skill, but it also reveals and reinforces our culture: we are dedicated to continually improve our performance. People who don't have much to say in team meetings probably didn't do the exercise, and that's why the notes are important.

Harvest success stories from people each week and prepare them to share their stories in team meetings. Keep track of who presents and make sure to get around to everyone on the team. Remember that even the people who might be perceived as weaker players can build their skills and experience success and recognition if their manager knows how to coach skills and write strong MAPs.

In team meetings or one-on-one meetings, ask participants to share their advice for successfully building specific sales skills. This is a form of recognition. Praise any effort, especially from those who may be a little resistant, reluctant, or lack confidence. Public compliments are very powerful.

MAPs are designed specifically to re-engineer behavior in such a way that everyone feels good about it, because the MAP is achieved within hours and immediately begins having a positive impact on agent habits, the customer experience, and business outcomes.

MAP – 3 Discovery Questions

On my next 20 calls I will ask at least 3 discovery questions about what the customer wants and why. I will make 3 check marks in each box and write down a word representing the customer's "why".

1 ✓ ✓ ✓ new job	2 ✓ ✓ ✓ relocating	3 ✓ ✓ ✓ first child	4	5
6	7	8	9	10
11	12	13	14	15
16	17	18	19	20

Figure 11.5   Map Tracker Notes

Don't Overwhelm

As far as we know, there is no law that says a coach has to give feedback on every single area of opportunity noted in a call. Don't coach or give feedback on too many behaviors simultaneously. You might think that would be more efficient, but it's not. It is less efficient because it lacks focus; lack of focus results in little or no behavior change; little or no change results in the sales manager coaching the same things over and over again, which is frustrating for both parties. It all adds up to a colossal waste of time and energy. Instead, pick the most important; or, if you are using a call guide/conversation guide, start at the top and work down, one behavior at a time.

Use Questions to Coach

One of the most important methods for motivating and teaching adult learners is the Socratic method. In Socrates' view, the philosopher's job is to ask the right questions to help people remember what they already know. With this method, the teacher uses a series of questions to help people discover and acknowledge values they already share. It is empowering because, when answering questions, the student becomes the teacher and the teacher becomes the student. Therein lies the secret of John Wooden's "providing correction without stirring resentment." Consider the examples below, one in a "telling" style and one in a Socratic, or "asking" style.

Telling Style Example

Sales manager: I want everyone to sit up straight when you greet the caller today and sound like you are interested and happy to help the person. I want to hear it on every call today, all right?

Team: Okay coach.

Asking Style Example (Call Coaching)

Sales manager: What do you think your voice sounds like when you are tired at the end of the shift and all hunched over your desk?

Salesperson: Probably not very good.

Sales manager: Who wants to give us a bad-way demo on what that might sound like?

Team member (sounding half asleep): Thank you for calling ACME. (Laughter ensues)

Sales manager: Have you ever talked to someone, when you were the customer, who sounded like that?

Team member: Yeah. Every time I call the utility company.

Sales manager: How does that make you feel?

Team member: Not only do they not care about me, they resent the fact I am calling them!

Sales manager: What kind of impression do you want to make on our customers?

Team member: Friendly, but professional and happy to help.

Sales manager: How do you manage to do that at the end of the day when you are tired? What advice would you give?

Sales manager: Who wants to give us a good-way demo on what that might sound like?

Team member (sounding friendly but professional and happy to help): Thank you for calling ACME, my name is Marge, what's yours?

Sales manager: Great demonstration, thank you! Now turn to the person next to you and practice your best greeting.

Sales manager (after practicing): So, who's committed to delivering an awesome first impression this afternoon?

Sales team members: We are!

Recognize People

"I see you." Humans have a deep need to be appreciated, and to feel affiliated with others. Paying compliments not only makes people feel good about what they are doing, it also builds their commitment to the cause (Ariely 2016). Compliments are also a gateway to influence. They build trust and rapport because the person being complimented feels liked. In turn, they trust that the person who (demonstrably) likes them will act in their best interest (Cialdini 2007).

What is the difference between a robust compliment and a weak one? Weak compliments lack detail. For example: "Nice job with that customer" or "Good work today." These examples don't really recognize what happened, or what difference it made in the world. Here is a better example that includes what the person did and what the impact was: "I really liked the way you listened patiently to that customer because she felt so relieved once she knew you were really listening. You set a great example for our team. Thank you!"

Fly-By Compliments

In a contact center one has the opportunity to observe performance all day long just by walking around. That means there are unlimited opportunities to notice and reinforce positive behaviors. As an option, you can apply the "asking style" when paying a compliment.

Coach (on one knee next to the agent): I'd like to pay you a compliment! You have a wonderful greeting today. I have to ask you, what is your technique, or how do you do it so well and so consistently?

Team member: I'm slowing my pace, using their name more often, and trying to have a pleasant inflection that doesn't sound like a crabby DMV clerk yelling "Next!"

Coach: That is so interesting. Let me ask you, in your experience, what is the impact on the customer when you do those things?

Team member: The calls start out better and continues that way, because even if they come in with an edge, my goal is to be the most pleasant part of their day.

Coach: What advice would you give to your peers on how to be as effective as you are?

Team member: I think your greeting is like the first line in a play, the first note in a concert. It's the first impression that sets the tone, so I deliver a conscious performance. Try one thing at a time, starting with slowing down on the inbound greeting.

Coach: Thank you for delivering an outstanding customer experience, and for setting a great example for the rest of the team. Can I depend on you to continue to do that?

Team member: All day!

Complimentary Tips

- Send a complimentary email to someone's manager and the manager will probably forward it on to the person you complimented.
- Say something complimentary about one person to another person while they are standing nearby; they will overhear the compliment and feel proud.
- Send someone else to ask their advice and they will feel respected.
- Recognize someone in a team meeting and they will feel appreciated.
- Ask someone's advice and they will know you value their opinion. Do it in front of other people for peer recognition and added impact.
- In a seated team meeting, go around the room to each team member and ask people to write down something they admire and appreciate about each person. After you go around the room, give the written compliments to the people who were complimented. After each person gets their written compliments, they hand them all to a person seated next to them, who reads each one aloud.

Calibrate

Most call centers hold regular call calibrations to ensure that managers are consistent in the way they evaluate calls. Typically, call calibrations include quality assurance and sales managers, but sometimes just one or the other. If it is a vendor situation, the client would also participate to take a pulse on what is happening on the front lines and what level of consistency they are getting in terms of customer service or sales processes. Best practices for call calibrations include:

- Ensure the tools you are using (e.g. scoresheets) effectively measure sales effectiveness. If not, get more tools.
- Assuming you have a sales process that includes the beginning, middle, and end of a call, go around the table and have different participants debrief different parts of the call, for example, the opening, discovery, solution, concerns, and close.
- Check for calibration, questions, and ambiguities. Come to consensus on the proper evaluation of the call.
- Spend only half of the allotted time on call listening and analysis. Spend the other half (a) coming to consensus on the #1 coaching priority based on that call; (b) identifying an effective micro action plan for the agent; and (c) rehearsing the agent coaching session. When you do this, the leadership team calibrates not only on the call, but also on the coaching.

Agent-Level Call Calibrations

Many contact center teams hold regular manager calibrations, but they do not hold agent-level team calibrations. We believe that team calibrations are a highly effective way to develop sales acumen, a learning and coaching culture, and future sales managers. As an option, you could score calls just like the manager calibrations. Another alternative is to select sections of calls rather than complete calls. It is usually a needle-in-the-haystack situation to find "perfect calls," but it is not difficult to find a wonderful greeting, an insightful discovery process, or an artful response to a customer with objections. You can make sourcing these highlights easier by coaching your reps to notify you when they've done something exemplary. You can pull the call and play part of it for the team, creating a library of top performance over time.

Takeaway Questions

Below are questions you can use for further reflection.

Takeaway Discussion Questions for Your Organization

- Do you provide for both scored and non-scored interactions?
- Does the quality assurance form effectively capture sales and customer service skills? If not, what can you do about it?

Takeaway Questions for Personal Reflection

- Is it possible you could increase your ratio of positive feedback to constructive feedback?
- How can you implement "one thing at a time" into your coaching?

12

Sales Enablement Best Practices

PEOPLE USE THE term "sales enablement" in many different ways. Here we are focusing on some of the capabilities and best practices that deliver the biggest benefits for both frontline and senior sales managers. All of the capabilities described below can be implemented separately, or you can subscribe to a platform that offers some combination.

Micro Learning

Whether you need to change the tail-light on your car, tune a guitar, or change your pranked iPhone from Korean back to English, you can learn how to do just about anything on YouTube within about 5 minutes. We have all come to expect that, because it is on-demand and highly efficient. Sales training today should be just the same when deploying e-learning or video.

Video

We believe that the core of sales management is sales coaching. Much of this book talks about how to deliver skills training in face-to-face situations. It's about explanation, demonstration, practice, and repetition. Video is one of the most impactful technologies to have come out of sales enablement so far. If you have budget, you can subscribe to one of the sales coaching video platforms. If not, you can use a share site or even email.

If you attempt to implement a commercial video coaching platform, be aware of three ways in which it can fail: (a) sales leadership does not hold salespeople accountable to submit their videos; (b) sales leadership does not hold sales managers accountable for reviewing the video submissions and providing timely feedback; (c) sales managers cannot provide competent feedback because they don't know the skills themselves. Make sure you have those ducks in a row and your video initiative will be a screaming success.

We recommend using video in several ways.

Video Rehearsal

First, you select a skill and record a video of a top performer demonstrating the skill. Next, learners receive an email inviting them to participate in a video rehearsal. They view a demonstration of a sales skill and a job aid that displays the sales process at play in the video demonstration. Their assignment is to record themselves demonstrating the same skill. If they're unsatisfied with a take, they can delete it and do it over. We know that, on average, salespeople will record themselves seven times before submitting a final version. Seven times! Until now, the only way we knew of to get a salesperson to do 10 push-ups was if we were in the same room with them. This is a game-changer, because people practice their skills independently, but we have access to the end result. Upon submission, the video will be reviewed by the sales manager who will provide feedback via video. If the performance is suboptimal, they can do it again. The best videos can be put on a leaderboard to establish a reference library of top performers.

You can also use video to record two people conducting a video rehearsal remotely. The person who is submitting the video will record themselves as usual, but they will bring in a partner on speakerphone or video chat (on a separate device). Think about how precise the sales coaching activities are that we have described in this book. Everything is broken down into its parts and then reassembled. When rehearsal activities fail, it is usually because there was not enough precision in the sales process, the scenario, the instructions, and the amount of time allocated. Keep it crisp.

Assessments and Certifications

When using video for rehearsal, you can give the salesperson an unlimited number of attempts and they upload the version they're satisfied with. But you can also use it in a different mode in which they only get one chance. This is more suited to a certification or final assessment. If you have your sales process broken down effectively, you can certify your salespeople on every skill using video.

Sales Manager and Marketing Channels

Another way to use video is to give private channels to sales leaders so they can send out messages to the troops whenever they want to. Some managers send personal welcome/thank you videos to new customers. We also recommend using it for product and market updates.

Micro Learning Delivery

Because video is so fast and easy to make, it opens up the number of teachers and coaches you can leverage throughout the organization. Top-performing salespeople can demonstrate skills and share success stories and best practices. Product people can give the latest updates, and marketing people can let the salespeople know what they are doing to generate leads.

Web Conferencing and Video Chat

We take these tools for granted, but they are powerful sales management tools if you manage a remote team. Web conferencing can be used for huddles, team meetings, and goal-setting meetings. Video chat can be used for check-ins and remote skill development training. If your remote team is in the habit of using audio-only conference calls, consider making the switch to video conferences.

Competency Assessment Tools

Back in the horse and buggy days, we did not really use sales competency models, but they were implied in the learning objectives for sales training. In other words, if you could perform all the sales skills in the field or on the phone, then you were competent. It's extremely helpful, however, to document your competency model because it then serves as the single source of truth for the sales process and its application in different scenarios, quality assurance standards for contact centers, the sales coaching rubric, the ongoing sales training agenda, and sales readiness assessments.

Where do competencies come from? They are the behaviors known to drive optimal sales results. We typically look at competencies in terms of four buckets: our customers and markets; our company and products; sales technology and strategy; and sales skills. Each competency is broken down into five levels. The desired level of competence across the sales force is a three. Anyone scoring below three in any area will be assigned learning activities to close the gap. People who emerge at levels four and five are flagged as mentors.

Scoring takes place periodically, for example annually, biannually, or quarterly. Both the salesperson and the sales manager rate the salesperson on each competency and then have a conversation about the results. You can imagine that these conversations are impactful because they highlight the differences in perception between the salesperson and the sales manager, and they challenge the sales manager to be precise about what constitutes competence. Periodic assessments produce a heat map across the sales organization. You can use this data to drive the training agenda for regional or national sales meetings and for creating micro learning.

If you implement a competency assessment tool, be prepared for the fact that it will force salespeople and sales managers to calibrate. Let's face it, whatever sales process and methodology you promote at your company, there's probably a spectrum of adoption. In other words, some people use all of it, some people use none of it, and there are a whole lot of salespeople in between. If you're going to create a sales competency model, it is best to bring your sales managers and top-performing salespeople in at the very start to document those competencies. If you do it this way, you'll have less calibrating to do on the back end.

Field Coaching Tools

Contact centers use online quality assurance tools, and in this book we have pictured printed forms for documenting performance feedback. For field sales, we recommend using a phone- or tablet-based performance feedback tool that captures the scenario, circumstance, or type of sales call and the salesperson's performance through each phase of the customer interaction. The benefit of doing this electronically rather than on paper is that it brings all the results together in one place so that once again, as with the assessment tool described above, you can see the heat map of opportunities. You can compare your salespeople to one another. You can do some trend analysis and see if they're making improvements. Senior sales leaders get visibility into the quality and quantity of coaching that is being delivered by their sales managers. Once again, this forces a moment of truth in which the sales management team has an opportunity to calibrate on expectations.

Machine Learning/Artificial Intelligence

Machine learning/artificial intelligence are in the early stages when it comes to analyzing and coaching sales performance, but very promising. Audio-analysis of telephone calls reveal factors that impact sales performance. For example, rate of speech, percentage of time spent talking vs. listening, verbal ticks, and even emotional analysis. You can also search recorded calls for keywords, so you can drill down into multiple conversations where specific topics were discussed. A sales manager can use this data to provide coaching, but a salesperson could also use the data to improve their own performance. For example, research from the Gong company across millions of calls reveals that lower-performing salespeople increase their rate of speech when they encounter an objection. In other words, they get nervous, they speed up, and they are less effective at overcoming the concern. Top-performing salespeople do the exact opposite. When the customer raises an objection, they go into slow motion because they are seeking first to understand, and they are confident in the response they will bring about once they have given the customer a chance to express themselves freely.

Analytics

How do you measure the return on investment for sales training and coaching? In a contact center it is relatively easy. Everyone is in one place and can be observed at any time. You can select a pilot group, train them, and coach them to competence with the types of activities we've described in Chapter 11 as well as throughout the rest of the book. In field sales it can be a little more difficult. Analytics dashboards provide the ability to plot learning activities against sales results. This allows you to analyze questions like: "Do salespeople become more effective when they receive more coaching? Which managers drive the best results from their coaching? What do they do differently in terms of the mix of coaching activities, and the manner in which they do them? What other learning activities (e.g. video rehearsals or watching top-performer best-practice videos) have the biggest positive impact on results?"

Takeaway Questions

Below are questions you can use for further reflection.

- Which of the following sales enablement best practices would most benefit your sales team? How could you implement them?
  - Video rehearsal.
  - Video assessments/certifications.
  - Video channels.
  - Micro learning.
  - Video conference and video chat.
  - Competency assessment tool.
  - Field coaching tool.
  - Machine learning/AI.
  - Analytics.

Appendix: Sales Coaching Cadences

THROUGH THE BOOK we have referenced three types of sales teams (field, inside sales, and contact center) and the sales coaching activities they benefit from most (review and plan meetings, goal-setting meetings, skill development training, sales meetings, sales huddles, and performance feedback). The frequency of these activities varies depending on the type of team. Below is an example coaching cadence for each type of sales team.

The field sales cadence is based on a calendar month and displays a monthly goal-setting meeting (with each salesperson), a team huddle on Monday mornings, a sales meeting every Friday, performance feedback twice a month, and check-ins a couple of times per week.

The inside sales cadence is similar but has weekly performance feedback, since everyone is presumed to either be in one location or have live monitoring or recorded calls available if remote.

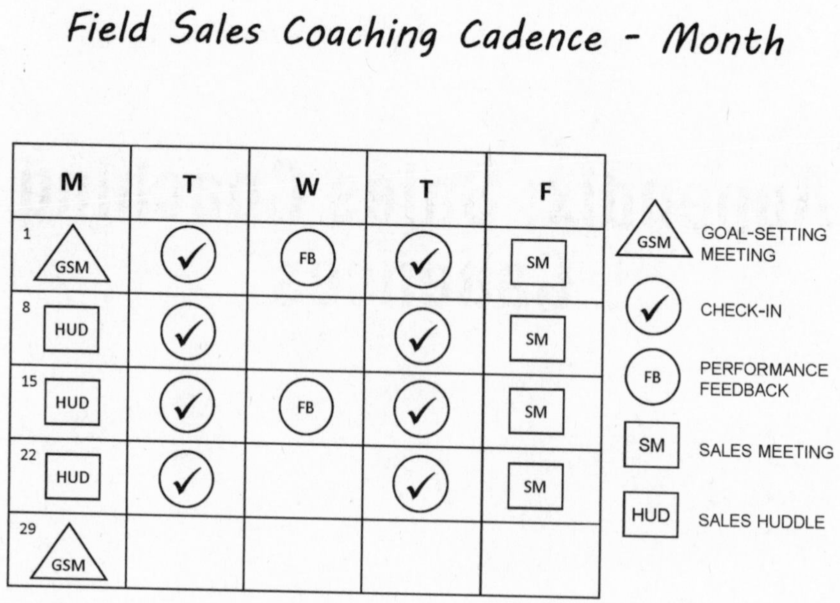

Field Sales Coaching Cadence - Month

Figure A.1   Field Sales Cadence

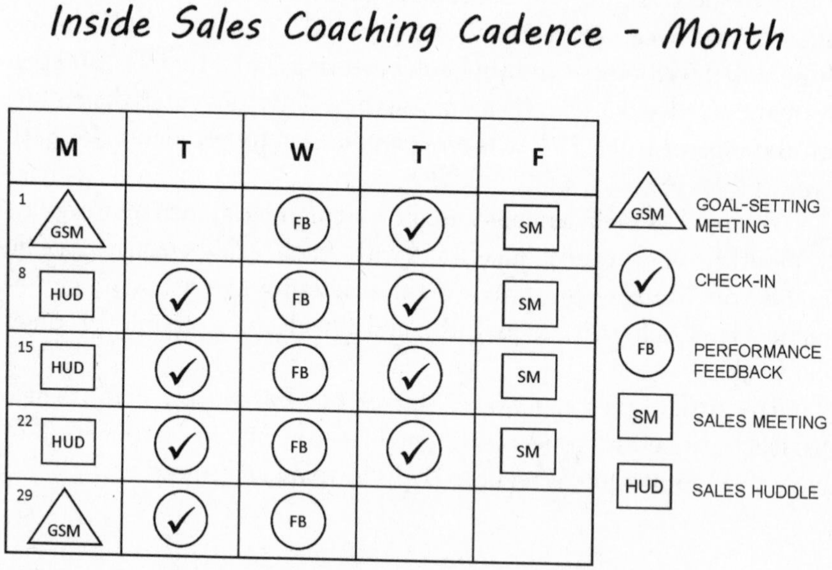

Inside Sales Coaching Cadence - Month

Figure A.2   Inside Sales Cadence

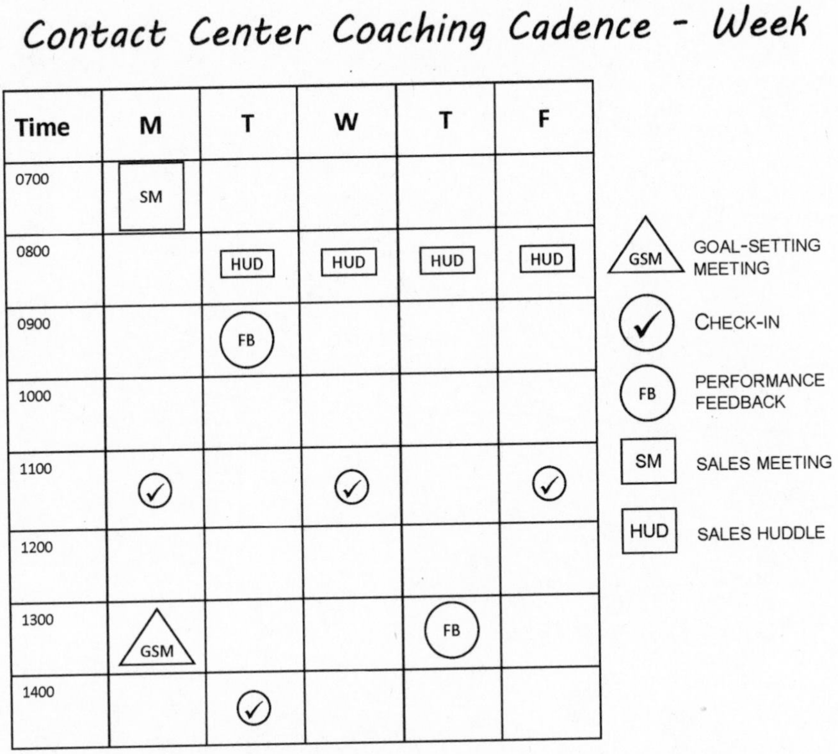

Contact Center Coaching Cadence - Week

Time	M	T	W	T	F
0700	SM				
0800		HUD	HUD	HUD	HUD
0900		FB			
1000					
1100	✓		✓		✓
1200					
1300	GSM			FB	
1400		✓			

GSM   GOAL-SETTING MEETING

✓   CHECK-IN

FB   PERFORMANCE FEEDBACK

SM   SALES MEETING

HUD   SALES HUDDLE

Figure A.3   Contact Center Cadence

The contact center cadence is based on one week, with a weekly goal-setting meeting, daily huddles, a weekly sales meeting, performance feedback twice a week (per agent), and check-ins on the alternating days.

References/Further Reading

Ariely, D. 2016. *Payoff*. New York: Simon & Schuster.

Cialdini, R. 2007. *Influence: The Psychology of Persuasion*. New York: HarperCollins.

Clifton, J. and Harter, J. 2019. *It's the Manager*. New York: Gallup.

Colvin, G. 2010. *Talent is Overrated*. New York: Portfolio/Penguin.

Miller Heiman Group. 2019a. "CSO Insights 2019 Sales Enablement Report." Available at https://www.csoinsights.com/wp-content/uploads/sites/5/2019/11/CSO-Insights-5th-Annual-Sales-Enablement-Study-3.pdf

Miller Heiman Group. 2019b. "All That Glitters Is Not Gold: Key Findings from the CSO Insights 2019 World-Class Sales Practices Study." Available at https://www.millerheimangroup.com/resources/resource/all-that-glitters-is-not-gold-results-of-the-2019-world-class-sales-practices-study/

Perlow, L. A., Hadley, C. N. and Eun, E. 2017. "Stop the meeting madness." *Harvard Business Review*, July–August.

Pink, D. H. 2009. *Drive*. New York: Riverhead Books/Penguin Random House.

Sinek, S. 2009. *Start with Why*. New York: Portfolio/Penguin.

Sinek, S. 2014. *Leaders Eat Last*. London: Penguin Random House.

Acknowledgments

Steve's Acknowledgments

Thanks to my wife, Elisa, and our children, Matthew and Anna, who have been very supportive of me over the last 20 years. They are a constant reminder of what life is really about: family. I also do not want to forget to mention our dog, Buster. I would not be who I am today without my Mom and Dad, Al and Donna Johnson, who were two exemplary role models in many ways – through their commitment to each other, their work ethic, and their values. They knew the way, went the way, and showed the way!!! All I had to do was follow!

Thanks to Matt Hawk for being the catalyst for this book. Without you I don't think I would ever have gotten this book done on my own. Elaine Jordan, you have been instrumental in the success of virtually every major endeavor we have undertaken at The Next Level in the last 10 years. As a company we would not be where we are today without you, and your support in finishing this book will never be forgotten.

I also wanted to thank the rest of our team here at The Next Level who I have been very fortunate to work with: Eric Gist, Mark Norman, Scott Laun, Gene St. Pierre, and Jack Litzelfelner. Thank you to the team at Wiley for your help and guidance. Finally, thank you to all of our clients at The Next Level – too many to mention. If it were not for you, we would not be who we are today.

Matt's Acknowledgments

We learn together. Thank you to all of the colleagues, clients, and mentors below, from whom, and with whom, I've learned everything I know about sales, sales training, and sales coaching: Alex Greengold, Bob Davis, Brian Ingles, Brian Lowery, Brian Quinn, Bronwyn Droog, Caroline Rhodes, Christopher Tracy, Craig Grunig, Dan Fitzsimmons, Dan Garner, Dan Heydenfeldt, Dave Palmer, Dennis Klemp, Dennis Reno, Diane Risk, Donnie Evans, Eneida Grunig, Eric Swanson, Frank Strauss, G.A. Bartick, Gary Fackett, Glory Weeks, Gordon Cooke, Dr. Howard B. Lewis, Jack Litzelfelner, Jay Tyler, Jeremy "Boomer" Stockton, Joe Galvin, Joe Trabuco, John Courtney, John Rooney, Joshua Cage, Juli Heydenfeldt, Julie Thomas, Kent McDougall, Leelah Huerta, Lori Lipke, Mark Norman, Michael "Mr." Hatt, Mike Dodge, Morrie Norman, Dr. Nate Brooks, Nancy Rael, Pat Scallon, Paul Ironside, Rich Eldh, Rod Johnson, Ron Coleiro, Scott Laun, Scott MacDonald, Sean Austin, Steve DeCamillo, Stuart Chant, Suzy Wieser, and Tom Karinshak.

Thanks to my unmatched colleagues at CareCredit, who – through ceaseless innovation and unwavering collaboration – drive the sales enablement engine: Adam Schricker, Amber Medina, Bete Johnson, Bethany Weeby, Brian Brister, Chuck Osburn, Courtney Vaughn, Crista Sampson, Christina Edwards, Fernando Campos, Dan Judkins, Danny Williams, Deena McCaig, Doug Hammond, Doug Voeks, Gaelle Bouteloup, Gina Gabrielson, Glen Holden, Grace Valle, Greg Pierce, James Frees, Jay Bonner, Jean Moody, Jena Ellsworth, Juan Aguero, Kris Jackson, Krissy Michaels, Laura Andrews, Leslie Potts, Leticia Romo, Marcus Proctor, Margarita Garza, Michael Kimbell, Randy Best, Robert McLinn, Rocio Hurtado, Scott Elias, Sharon Daugherty, Sharon Tye, Shirley Misiak, Todd Stevens, Valerie Lando, and Victor Aellos. To Gary Reiter, who for nearly 20 years has been my client, my manager, my coach, and my friend. Thank you all for the incredibly rewarding journey.

I want to acknowledge my friend, mentor, co-author, and force of nature, Steve Johnson, without a doubt the most "seasoned salesman" to ever knock on every door in Los Angeles. A long time ago, you gave me a chance as an apprentice and started me on a path to mastery.

When I faltered at first, you didn't give up on me. Thank you for the investment you made.

Thanks to all the other educators and authors in my family for leading the way: William A. Hawk and Marian Hawk, Lisa S. Hawk and Betsy R. Cassriel, Dana Rheinschmidt, Steve Rheinschmidt, and Frank Smith.

Thanks to my wife, Lisa R. Hawk, a brilliant sales manager in her own right, my high-school sweetheart, and still number one in my heart. And thanks to our children, Sarah, Tyler, and Benjamin. You inspire me every day. You know how to learn, you know how to lead, you know how to love, you are unstoppable.

About the Authors

Steve Johnson is the founder and president of The Next Level Sales Consulting, whose goal is to help their clients improve their bottom-line sales performance. Steve has been on over 7,000 face-to-face sales meetings and has made over 150,000 calls to schedule meetings, follow up, and close sales. (You can tell by looking at him he has been rejected 143,000 times.) In the last 35 years he has trained over 10,000 sales managers, over 90,000 salespeople, and created over 800 customized programs. Steve is the co-author of the 1996 LA Times bestseller *If You're Not Out Selling, You're Being OutSold* and the 2006 Amazon.com bestseller *Selling is Everyone's Business*.

Matt Hawk, Ph.D. is a consultant and Vice President of Instructional Design and Training Delivery at Synchrony. He began his sales career at Gartner, selling to technology vendors, and later managed the sales team for US Interactive during the dot-com era. From 2004 to 2017 he sold, developed, and implemented dozens of customized performance improvement programs in the USA, Canada, Mexico, the Philippines, India, and Brazil for sales managers and their teams at Fortune 500 companies through the sales training companies he founded, Retention Specialists and Customer Loyalty Specialists. Matt earned his doctorate from Yale University and is a member, contributing author, and speaker on the topic of sales enablement for the Association for Talent Development.

Index